T0290441

David Rigsbee does not promise mending, bu [...]
work of connection.
—Sarah Lindsay

David Rigsbee gives us stunning moments; he draws us under the deep water.
—Ann Marie Macari

David Rigsbee's poems offer as premise and example a sensitivity at once tautly
responsible and generous.
—Jordan Smith

Few other poets so powerfully capture both the ignorant cruelty and profound
love we bear one another.
—Peter Makuck

This is the voice of the American southern raconteur—musical, thoughtful,
discursive, political. I'm drawn to the honesty of its unhurried recollections and
its steady intelligence to its longings and angers and the twinkle in its eye.
—Dorianne Laux

One can only hope a lot of people have time and leisure to experience poems as
accomplished, multitudinous, complicated and evocative.
—Andrew Glaze

David Rigsbee is one of our indispensable poets.
—Fred Chappell

Rigsbee's poems are, above all else, quests. They are searches for meaning and
endless haunts for an explanation, and they look not with envy but with grief at
the more uncomplicated forms—flies, bears, tulips, sustaining *their* own lives.
His poems are stubbornly honest and delicate, and I am moved by them.
—Gerald Stern

David Rigsbee's poems chart the shifting geographies, the oceanic flux, of the
human spirit. Like the maps of master cartographers, they engage the world
while leading us toward vast privacies, what remains nameless.
—Michael Waters

Rigsbee's tensile imagination takes on an air of achievement through the very
strength and energy with which he makes the poem move.
—David Ignatow

www.blacklawrence.com

Executive Editor: Diane Goettel
Cover Design: Zoe Norvell
Cover Art: untitled © Jill Bullitt
Book Design: Amy Freels

Copyright © David Rigsbee 2024
ISBN: 978-1-62557-063-5

All rights reserved. Except for brief quotations in critical articles or reviews, no part of this book may be reproduced in any manner without prior written permission from the publisher: editors@blacklawrencepress.com.

Published 2024 by Black Lawrence Press.
Printed in the United States.

WATCHMAN IN THE KNIFE FACTORY

New & Selected Poems

DAVID
RIGSBEE

Books by David Rigsbee

Poetry:
MAGA Sonnets by Donald Trump, Main Street Rag, 2021
This Much I Can Tell You, Black Lawrence Press, 2017
School of the Americas, Black Lawrence Press, 2013
The Pilot House, Black Lawrence Press, 2011
The Red Tower: New & Selected Poems, University of Georgia Press, NewSouth
     Books, 2010
Two Estates, Cherry Grove Collections, 2009
Cloud Journal, Turning Point, 2008
Sonnets to Hamlet (chapbook), Pudding House, 2004
The Dissolving Island, BkMk Press, University of Missouri at Kansas City, 2003
Greatest Hits: 1975—2000 (chapbook), Pudding House, 2001
Scenes on an Obelisk (chapbook), Pudding House, 2000
A Skeptic's Notebook: Longer Poems. St. Andrews Press, 1997
Your Heart Will Fly Away, The Smith, 1992
The Hopper Light, L'Epervier Press, 1988
To Be Here. Coraddi (chapbook), 1980
Stamping Ground, Ardis, 1976

Editorial:
The Ardis Anthology of New American Poetry. Ardis, 1977
An Answering Music: On the Poetry of Carolyn Kizer, Ford-Brown & Company, 1990
Invited Guest: An Anthology of Twentieth Century Southern Poetry, University of
     Virginia Press, 2001

Translation:
Dante: Paradiso (translation), Salmon Poetry, 2023

Prose:
Not Alone in My Dancing: Essays and Reviews, Black Lawrence Press, 2015
Styles of Ruin: Joseph Brodsky and the Postmodernist Elegy, Greenwood Press, 1999
Trailers, University of Virginia Press, 1996

Contents

New Poems

Joan   3

Storm   5

The Innocence   8

Good Friday, 2018, Driving South   9

Reenactors   11

I Will Meet You There   12

Executor   14

Red Wall   15

Poem in August   16

Goodwill   18

Interdiction   20

The Thousand Acres   21

Bluefish   22

Why We Marry   24

from *This Much I Can Tell You* (2017)

January   29

A Certain Person   30

Max and the Promise   31

Oversize Load   33

This Much I Can Tell You   36

'68   37

Clothespins   39

Armature   41

The Takeaway   42

Falsetto   43

Ten-Second Delay 45
Empire Service 47
Unfriend Me 48
Composition 49
Helmets 50
Infidel 51
Miss Tilley 52
Out of the Past 54
Dream Baby 56
As If 58
On a Line from CK 60
Stay 61
The Red Dot 63
The Porch 66
The King of Thebes 67
A Breakfast 69
The Earwig 70
Not the Mighty but the Weak 71

from *School of the Americas* (2012)

Shum 75
Canoe 77
In Passing 78
North State 80
The Stegosaurus 81
Charlotte Mew 83
The Hook 84
Field Service Report 86
Gil's Sentence 87
Redcaps 89

Roy Orbison, New Orleans, 1984   90
Get It Down   92
Mink   93
Talking Points   95
Russians   96
I Am Nobody   97
The Assassination of Sadat   98
At the Grave of Jesse Helms   100
Masha   102
Sodomites   104
Elsewhere   106
The Attic   107
Ode to Wilbur Mills   109
Treehouse   111
After All   112
Magic Marker   115
School of the Americas   116
Song for Tom   118
Bald Man with Poodles   120
Heresies of Self-Love   121
The Slug   124
The Courage of Unspeakable Acts   126
The Translator   128
Yes Way   129
Dalman Flowers   131

from *The Red Tower* (2010)
A Life Preserver   135
Harp   136
Roofers   137

Rorty   138
The Apartment   139
The Ferry   140
The Red Tower   141
Theology   142
Thinking about Logan   143

from *The Pilot House* (2009)
After Reading   147
Patience   148
Lincoln   149
The Gulf   150
The Pilot House   151
Wised Up   152
Moulin   153
The Contest   154
Immortal Soul   155

from *Two Estates* (2009)
At Todi   159
Never Forget   160
Into the Wall   161
Campanile   162
Vespers   163
Combine Stopped in a Field   164
Gate by a Boat Pond   166
Houses in a Necropolis   167
Engraver's Stone   168
Annunciation   169

Not the Tall Grass 170
The Landscapist 171
Qua 172
Mowing Day 173
Piero's Resurrection 174
Lemon Trees near Izzalini 176
Luna Park 177
Necropolis near Fiore 178
Of a Party 179
Secret Hours 180
Realm of Day 181
Falling Giottos 183
Uncrossed Passes 184
Poem at Midsummer 185
Terra Cotta 186
Air Traffic 187
Wind Picking Up 188
Discontinued Subjects 189
Ellipsis 190
Scenes on an Obelisk 191
Such as Stone 192
Sun on Stucco 193
Terraces 194
The Digs 195
The Temple 196
The Thrush 197
Under Cancer 198
Untitled Landscape 199
After Rain 200

A Suburb Away   201
Bar Gianicolo   202
End of Sight   203
Frescoes Underground   204
On the Way to the Basilica   205

from *Cloud Journal* (2008)
from Sonnets to Hamlet   209
from Cloud Journal   216

from *The Dissolving Island* (2003)
The Garden of Catherine Blake   223
The Metaphysical Painters   224
The Tufted Grosbeak   225
A Dawn   226
Almost You   228
Dream Oration   229
Ex Ponto   231
Fault Line   233
Grayscale   235
Heat   237
Hosanna   239
In Memory of James Broughton   241
Kiefer, the First Day of Spring   242
Linking Light   244
My Raven   245
Only Heaven   247
Safe Box   248
Sketches of Spain   249

Spaghetti   251
Stefano   254
The Dissolving Island   255
The Exploding Man   257
Turner's Mists   259
Umbrian Odes   261
Wild Strawberries   268

from *A Skeptic's Notebook: Longer Poems* (1996)
Leaving Old Durham   273
Suite for Susan Rankaitis   281
Four Last Songs   296

from *Your Heart Will Fly Away* (1992)
Anymore   315
Atomic Future   317
Autobiography   320
Bermudas   322
Buried Head   325
Collected Poems   327
Crickets   328
God's Tumbler   329
La Bohème   333
Mozart   334
Secondary Road   336
Stars in Leo   337
Sunbathing   339
The Mermaid   340
The Mountaintop   345

The Trawlers at Montauk   347
The Word "World" in Jarrell   348
White   350

from *The Hopper Light* (1988)
A Hanging   355
A Respectable Man   357
Caught in Rain   360
Cleaning Vegetables   362
Equinox   364
Giacometti's Dream   365
The Hopper Light   367
The Peacocks at Winter Park   369
The Stone House   371

Acknowledgments   373

for Cleopatra and Liliana

New Poems

Joan

It was no different than any other day.
Already, we were hyper-aware of the clock
whose poker-face ticked toward nine.

Our teacher was a clueless woman with her
upswept, stainless pussycat glasses,
slip strap inching down her sleeveless arm

as she diagrammed sentences that looked
like the cutaway of a ship, words on deck,
then all the way down to steerage.

The late student was a tall girl, Joan,
first heir of integration. I will not say
beneficiary, because it was the day

we tortured her. She seemed a lonely girl,
but it would be more correct to say our prank
only bolded the torment of her being

there, where she belonged, to learn
how language sought the measure,
to release her from the trap of thoughts

unexpressed. Someone had the brilliant
idea to bring a box of thumbtacks
and shared them with us before class.

We leaned over to pour three or four
like spilled candy on the oak desk seat.
Then we returned to our zits and waited,

staring at desktops, books closed.
She appeared, the teacher looked up,
said nothing, and returned to her chore.

Wishing to be invisible, Joan moved
among the seats, pulling the skirt of her
white dress aside to pass down the row

until she found her seat and looking up
at the gray teacher, sat. Color of plum.
Color of the internal sweetness fading,

the jolt of the joke revealed. All that
we could never know passed us then
the way a blanket of blackbirds

suddenly sweeps itself off the sweetgum
and scatters into the Carolina night,
leaving the leaves for a moment shaken.

For she was a child and we were children.

Storm

When they let us back on the island,
we could smell the devastation.
After the spiked chaos, the air
was unmoving, mysteriously stilled.

We found our place, a trailer, bisected
by a flayed yaupon trunk, whose missile
spewed insulation like Spanish moss.
You could step over the gash

into the kitchen, which was itself
waste now, rank and sopping as
the black swamp at the property's edge.
We peered in, but went no further.

Down the coast, guttural graders
grunted and shouldered piles
of construction dreck. It was as if
we had dreamt of the storm's slash,

the night in flood, but in our minds
the dark nation was itself awash.
As a child, I dashed like a sandpiper
along the changing, bubbling edge.

Daddy followed the newly hatched
turtles, swinging his baseball bat
at seagulls that swooped to pick off
strays from the awkward pilgrimage.

Not far from the sea, tobacco fields
grew lush and poisonous. Planters
having set the nascent yield in rows
stood in sheds, their harrows caked.

By late summer, the pickers came.
The toil grew monumental, though
there were no monuments, just tales
told nightly, exhaled from porches

about the tractors, planters,
weeders and toppers, tugging at buds,
mashing the hornworms, tossing them,
so the brightleaf could luxuriate.

It was the knot of factories,
farther inland that drew my old man
who took his steel toolbox to adjust
the massive machines from Germany,

always in need of calibration
so that the cigarettes rolling off
the hopper were uniform, practical
as pencils, appealing and smooth.

And so manufactured his end too,
when for a while we didn't know
he sped to the clinic to hook up
his IV with the other bald lungers.

The Corps idled by their trucks. No one
knew what to do. We turned and saw
a house inverted, settling into its own roof,
plumbing pipes like periscopes aimed

at the cloudless horizon. On either side
nothing remained but concrete rectangles,
then sand swooping like a hammock
to the scummed edge of the shore.

The stink lingered well into the cleanup.
Westward, the fields were flooded.
The sun rose on new lakes of stalks
just as it had on the ruined island,

the incognito landscape where we would
never return. It was "the storm of the century,"
the papers said, but no one was prepared
to say what calmed the engine of the sea.

The Innocence

"Jim Beam for me, not vodka!"
the Russian beauty caterwauled, hurling herself
into the living room of the safe house.
She swung the bottle like a censer
in front of my eyes and climbed onto my lap.
Her grandfather, a minister of Stalin, had survived
'38 and the war, and thus passed by agents
in three countries, she landed in Middle America
where she stared into my face with those
Russian eyes, decades ago, during the manifest
destiny of Gerald Ford. Already weaving
where she sat, trailing the edge of the bottle
against the parquet floor, she sank
her tongue into my startled mouth, then said,
a moment later, "I don't want to talk about Yesenin.
Let's drink this, then go to bed."
There were others present, geniuses among them,
but they were displaced on sofas
and love seats, while the wild girl
went about seduction, and I calculated
the possible outcomes. But I didn't comply
and she fell asleep, snoring in my arms.
The others scarcely turned and went about
their party while Carly Simon
crooned knowingly from the speaker.
Then I thought of the innocence of Russia,
of Blok's twelve apostles with their cigarettes and kvass,
of time unhinged from years, of Akhmatova
standing in line with gifts,
never delivered, for her rotten son.

Good Friday, 2018, Driving South

The day didn't alter its early monochrome.
By the time I got onto the pike
it was slicked with rain, and every passing car
renewed the brief but annoying mist,
swelling and subsiding, as cherry taillights
burned through, and you had to use the wiper
manually, until the rubber squeaked against the glass.
Spring had not yet come, despite the efforts
of early flowers clumped by austere trees
and the occasional faint bird call
that penetrated the cabin, a kind
of aimless searching, even echolalia.
But mostly I was aware of the motoring
monotony and the ebb and flow
of tires like a stadium far away, for which
it was impossible to determine who was winning,
only that it was taking place and someone was.
My thought turned to Donne, presenting
his wit to the Most High, as I always recalled
on that day. The thought led me to a friend
who used to speak of him as though he were present
and smirking over a pint at the tiny attempt
we made to register too, like dust on a lens.
And what if we didn't register? What if
we only clutched our dolor all the way down?
Many are the times I woke, rose,
and went forth in what felt like rebalancing
after a heavy dream or guideposts
through an uncanny countryside.
This time was eerily similar.

Hartford was awful, I thought, all
bottlenecked and yet devoid of citizens,
the sidewalks like bezels outlining sodden
public spaces, parks and self-doubting commercial zones.
The radio was no help, either repetitive and banal
or imposing and unrelenting: no middle way.
I wanted to connect the day to my experience,
but the weatherman had promised a smudge
of clouds, neither rising nor setting sun,
just hazy relations between cars
and the land, between cars and things.
Lacking shadow, I drove on south to Waterbury,
New Britain, Newtown, still in rain,
past the unremarkable exit sign to Sandy Hook,
to Danbury, and the New York line,
where I separated from the last of the pods.
For a moment, it was like stepping off a ledge
where everything rushes up to meet you,
only to turn, only to be done with you.

Reenactors

I remembered how, breaking from a silent
hospice vigil, my relatives reassembled and sat
like Confederate reenactors at a long table.
We had ordered, and heaped bowls arrived.
This being a restaurant for regulars, I noticed
older couples consisting of high-capped men
and demure women attending to their meals.
We were surrounded by only them.
Then one squirrelly provocateuse, an in-law,
turned to me and asked for a grace.
That it was a test was lost on no one,
their lowered eyes peering up to watch.
My urge was to rise and head for the exit
with imagined, prow-like dignity, leaving them,
I hope, stunned. Instead, I burrowed
inward and found the script of childhood,
which said, "I am you," saying grace
but also meaning, "I am not you,"
Not in pious helplessness, but in fact.
Something in the next moment did pull me,
and soon I was out of there, though I sat
and finished the meal, wiping my mouth
of the greasy pork, the slimy sweet coleslaw,
then tossing the napkin thankfully,
truly, onto the empty white plate.

I Will Meet You There

"I looked on the earth, and lo, it was waste and void;
and to the heavens, and they had no light."
—Jeremiah 4

There was a woman sitting in a coffee shop.
It was morning. She was with her latté.
She looked out the window, mostly street,
everything in motion in every direction.

She came back to her coffee, whose wisp
of steam issued from a small oval hole
in the plastic lid. Her brother was ascending
the elevator elsewhere. Emails awaited him,

and blue sky, which was not in view either there
or at the coffee shop, which nobody noticed anyway,
because it had sailed to the end of summer.
She tired already, thinking of her concluding chores,

among which was their mother, whose swelling
complaints they would prefer to avoid, but joined
to manage. And of the emails? One said,
"I will meet you there in the afternoon."

The distance was one mile. They had both
measured it once, sitting before a map,
like some kind of shared radiant thought.
There were coordinates, the kind siblings

shared like a supernatural gift, though no one
believed in such things. The sky was unchanged.
The wind pushed under the park trees, as you
would raise an elderly woman to take her pills.

Elsewhere another wind pushed at treetops
that swayed begrudgingly like the smokestacks
of early ships. No guy-wires fastened them,
and one day they would topple without ceremony.

Executor

In the box I expected, of course, evidence
of journeys, exotic, stony destinations
where her famous friends, those
with prizes and wit, waved on the dock
having come to greet her, a fellow traveler.
They would have adventures, diversions,
and engagements proper to their kind.
When they were home, such material!
Just like the tragedians and satirists.
When their books came out, they signed
them with abiding love, vigorous pledges
rendered in tiny, unassertive script.
From the first book, as with all
the others I quarried, flyers fell out:
reviews from *The Nation, Poetry,*
and *The New York Times Book Review.*
On the back page, notes, "P 150—Metaphor,"
"P 72—relation of present and past,"
"P 29–31—Barbarians." I reinserted
the reviews and returned the books
to their container, sealed it with masking tape,
careful that the creases were straight,
the tape itself reinforced and taut.

Red Wall

Consider the lintel: summer opens:
Aphrodite plus sparrows,
and hot stones the size of office safes.
Regardless, the past follows
like Melchior without makeup,
while a turtle slumbers on a stump.
Maple leaves squirm on their twigs
when an antic breeze bellies up
and through. Then the neighbor
with the black knee brace and that gait
drags her green bag to the curb.
The telephone poles, misaligned, trail off
behind the smaller trees, pulled in every direction,
steadied by thick wires anchored
in the prim, fussed-over lawns
where black-eyed Susans and sunflowers
stand up in their beds. So martyrs
were painted in Italy once, tethered
to their stakes, their upward eyes seeking
some sign of coherence from beyond
the canvas. Because the light seemed to come
from everywhere, I could see a brown spider
inch up a red wall, pause, and then turn to see
if there were not something there behind,
in pursuit, perhaps, before resuming
its trek up the layered shingles.

Poem in August

There was goodness in the time
of the hurricanes, houses blown to the stars,
the brutal sea.

There was goodness in the time
of my aunts and uncles, of all who crawled
over the soil,

the clouds connecting their small heads
to the horizon's hot beaches, the clouds
themselves amorphous

like goodness in the time you were born
before the shovels, before
the coming and going.

There was goodness too in the not-
goodness, the clutching at pills
spilled across the linoleum,

the children playing doctor
with roots and powders,
the mother who gobbled dirt,

so hungry was she for nutrients,
the baby thrown at a soldier,
all the falling.

It was the motor for the word,
the lovers who came unstuck
from each other and got up.

It was a locomotive for the sigh,
the whimper, the last breath
and what didn't come after.

There was goodness and there were
some who gathered their cardboard
and wrote poems that were

coordinates and messages by storefronts
where crowds lunged this way
and that

and the cars could barely move
in their steel and abundance,
there were so many.

Goodwill

"I already hear them speaking on the edge of my tomb.…
Already, yet when I will no longer be. As though
pretending to say to me, in my very own voice: rise again."
—Derrida

We slept by the dead man one room away.
There was hair in the wood. I put it in my wallet.

All felt smaller as I look down the corridor.
The radio said blizzard, and the ground

closed. These things. An old fellow had greeted
us at the door, his beard a gray cravat.

A stranger like the other stranger who called
in a soft, solicitous voice, to name, to say.

I have never figured out how to organize
these matters, but you understand

don't you? How the snow intervened, how
it was all planned in the morning that

by afternoon had turned to business,
mocked by the caged parrot who would

fall silent later, a florid Iago, until his widow
sold him. And how the children slipped away.

Who could hold on to their trembling bodies?
One into the army, one into the trade,

or so we feared. *We gotta get out of this place,*
wailed the oldies station to my pale parents

ignoring the mounting snow.
Things in the hills of West Virginia:

the mule deer, a bobcat making
a treble clef in the bare branch of a sycamore,

a hawk that had no purchase on heaven,
sitting hunched as Al Pacino watching

the escape of light. I had driven the highway
many times but only once did it bring anything

remotely approaching joy. My new wife
was at my side; there was no rot in sight.

We gathered and shook hands. The fireplace
joined us with its gas logs and puny flame.

We did not know what was opening before us.
It wasn't a tale. It was a blizzard at its

business, and time for the rest of us
to do what we do, meet, and part, and meet

again. And part, of course, into secluded
streets over the rise where night waited

with its abandoned clothes, its Goodwill, where
there is something for everybody, as I

have come to believe, that is the beginning,
for very little, of anything else.

Interdiction

There is only one thing to do
and that you cannot do.
The very thing, the life-giving thing,
and that you cannot do.
There is only one thing to say,
and that you cannot say.
The Erínyes wait, the nearest limb.
There is only one place to go
and you cannot go there.
Nor can you think it
without raising before you
the image: here sleep galls.
I was about to say "falls"
but the gods prevented me.
No falling. There is only one
thing you must look at,
and that you cannot see.
That you cannot see. Nor
will there be accommodation
for the hammering heart,
the empty lungs, the tongue.
They wait, talons tightening.
And what you cannot know
you know, and what is
intolerable you tolerate,
what is deathly you live for
to die for, until the tree is full.

The Thousand Acres

Two years back he was startled
to find her, and to find in himself
an opening in the rockslide debris.
But in a strange place of distances
and unfamiliar noises, she took him
by hand and led him up dry hills,
past herds of antelope and mule deer,
until they came to a windy prospect:
cattle-fence-bound valleys, hills in bunched
array, then smoothed into prairie, all
belted and parceled. They called it
The Thousand Acres. Here they sat
and stared out over the new world:
every horizon rimmed with mountains
already snow-topped, the whiteness
a filament not even thread, awaiting a tailor
of the imagination, maybe, and there was
no way to know that the first desire
that charged their bodies in nights
of love and days of friendship, like poetry
and prose together entering some canon,
contained a flaw none saw coming,
so high was the start of it, so long
the view. Just so philosophy routs
the striving poem, and what was classic
in the shape of desire tithes the clouds
and bows before the languorous
sweep of broad, impassive shadows.

Bluefish

A forgotten uncle surfaced in my memory
the other day when I got back from a walk
by the river. The family called him Bud, as if
you could expect him to come into his own
some springtime down the road.
In this way he came into maturity
still carrying simplicity at the same time.
He was uneducated, and yet his vivid way
with words matched his florid face.
"Them are stout buggers!" he would exclaim.
He actually pronounced them *boogers,* as he
pointed to the bluefish lining the pier's edge.
"That's some good eatin' there," he would add.
It was the kind of saying that emerged
as uncontested as a rhetorical question.
A fleet of clouds sailed overhead
followed by another, in pursuit.
These are my only literal quotes,
and so I associate him with fish, the way
the character in *As I Lay Dying* thought
his mother was a freshwater drum.
One day he toppled on the pier of a stroke,
passing out as his brain detonated,
and the other fishermen gathered around
the body, wondering what to do,
adjusting their caps and looking away
from time to time. There was nothing to do,
except to notify somebody. One of the men
peeled off and started walking, not running,
to the pier-house. Bud had wide blue eyes,

at canted angles, and a gap-toothed smile
that spread the endemic freckles of our clan.
The Atlantic shouldered in and the pier swayed,
bright clouds continued. Men stood about.
A wooden ship appeared in the distance,
then two, their sails and the clouds a rhyme.

Why We Marry

For Kurt Erickson and Heidi Moss

You see it when night returns
and you think, yes, I could have
stayed far away, but did not.
And the night rises steadily
to meet that small affirmative,
bringing with it smoky clouds
that will separate and reform
into a darkening monochrome,
according to the law.
Starlings race across the rooftops
as the west pulls the light after it.
You find the banter of birds pronounced,
each insisting on its rights.
A few peel off and fly upward
as if they wanted to see the curvature
of the earth. They remember
how it is, living the days in disbelief.
A man presents his torso to the window
and cars go by below, their missions
useless to speculate upon. Some kids
gather on the corner. One lights another's
cigarette. A third stares down, texting,
her face glowing. Or not unglowing,
and yet clear and not ungracious.
For the night moves each
into a renewed formation, the night
that contains the past, the way the soil
contains every single one of the dead.
Your hand extends on a day in the future.

Think of it like a small beetle, raising
its wing case with a flick, which is not
an announcement but a portion of silence,
pretending one thing,
and meaning the invisible other.

from
This Much I Can Tell You
(2017)

January

for Linda Gregg

Being a man, I was the least
among the shades
because of what I still carried.
I asked the caryatid to extend
her hand, but it was broken,
which is the way with stone.
There were several at the entrance,
but they were ornamental,
no longer load-bearing.
The dead would not have it.
The sun was sinking toward the rim,
I remember. I remember too
the poet said, it is more important
to walk across a field now
than to revisit the sorrows.

A Certain Person

It was Auden, I believe, who said that
in a certain person's presence he felt
"incapable of doing anything base
or unloving." Walking past the flat
on St. Mark's Place, past the memorial
plaque that, until this year, bore his name,
I look ahead to the park where
the homeless line up, as black squirrels
hop down from the leafless trees
to forage in the dry grass, the same
grass where a tiny mouse, rescued
from someone's sink and carried
in a clear, half-pint container, now roams,
if mice can be said to roam.
And persons capable of doing both base
and unloving things stroll across the bricks
the way they do in pictures of promenades
of foreign capitals between the wars.
The homeless line holds steady
all afternoon, and from a loudspeaker
somewhere comes the clarinet I take
to be Artie Shaw's. From somewhere else
Lil Wayne answers. Neither could be
described as without difficulty. Shaw,
for instance, was married eight times.
Where is the Auden plaque now?
It must be someplace, even if
it's no place. And when Shaw recorded
"Green Eyes," was there a mouse
in a sink somewhere wondering with his
tiny wit about the flatness and the whiteness
and the dark hole at the center?

Max and the Promise

"I had a dream of purity
and I have lived in the desert ever since."
—George Garrett

One day, Max Steele called me into his office
ostensibly to discuss short fiction,
but the news of Mishima's *seppuku*
had swept through the department
earlier that morning. I was a student
and as sensitive to literary rumors
and gossip as any bumblebee
riding the first spring breeze. Outside,
the SDS taunted the Young Republicans,
while frat boys in their Madras shorts
talked trash to passing hippies.
But in far-off Japan, after charging Mt. Fuji
in Nutcracker uniforms, the Shield Society
had drawn attention to the tiger's paw.
It was not enough to be a writer,
even reaching the Nobel stratosphere.
Only death would seal the deal,
only death reverse the dishonor,
heal the emasculation. So he prepared
in his Victorian house for years:
real death after role-playing,
ceremonial oblivion after deep hurt.
His last words before disembowelment
and beheading: "I don't think
they heard me very well." Max swung
around in his chair and said, "promise me
you'll never kill yourself!" Startled as I was,
I did. I saw Max in Nixon a few years later,

when we learned how the President
had led Kissinger to the carpet and prayers
in the Oval Office. I forgave Nixon
when I realized he was human, and I made
the gentle Max loosen his grip
when I saw how he, unlike his name,
fit so snugly in his little patch
of ground, a plaque commemorating
what forgetfulness routinely undoes.
Even Jesus would have failed
Max's oath: it's no wonder
such promises hold but for five minutes,
no wonder self-destruction mirrors
self-creation: how could it not?
Max lay long wasting before he died.
My niece torched herself in a motel room
at 18, prepared and afraid, having made
no promise to a teacher, embracing
self-immolation as the cure for love.
And then there was my brother.
I have seen the end of my rope
lying in a coil, and you couldn't tell
if it was a snake or a garden hose
or just a length of rope. Max and Mishima
are dust; the niece I never knew:
a picture. My brother, the silence
before and after the poem. All these
chapters feeding the effrontery and sorrow.
Empson admired a Buddha head
which was chiseled with a hooded cobra
risen in glory inches away and trained
to protect his double face.

Oversize Load

Of course, they left the "d" off.
People don't see the use
of the past participle anymore.
Perhaps they don't understand it,
its simple descriptive power.
Perhaps they have no feel for suffixes,
as for a thing grown irrelevant over time.
After all, docking the past
can be a good idea, sometimes.
I was fleeing depression that day
and headed out to the interstate.
I will not bore you with details.
There I listened to Roy Orbison
assault eternity with his high notes,
followed by the "55 Essential Tracks"
of The Everly Brothers. It was a lot
of emotion to cover, and the highway
seemed as good a place as any, since
the feeling of flight did its faultless
parody of transport and blended
with the changing landscape,
the humble farms transmogrifying
into the tacky suburbs that replaced them.
Before I knew it, I was over the state line
into Virginia, which I am reminded
is "for lovers," as the billboard
used to say. (*Only* for lovers, you
had to wonder?) The smaller truck,
the one with the bad grammar,
used flashing lights to keep creepers

at a distance. No worries: no one
was eager to pass, anyway.
What I couldn't yet process was
that there was another up ahead:
two pairs of trucks, each
with a smaller, trailing pickup
with revolving lights and that sign,
and before it, a squat semi, where
chained to each flatbed like Prometheus
after he had irked Zeus,
was a *tank*—an Abrams tank.
Twice I did a double-take
because what I could finally make out,
when I was pulling up closer,
was the barrel of the cannon, lowered
and trained squarely at me as I came on.
To what battles these were being sent
or returning—as is more likely—from,
there was no hint, only brown dirt
dried in the sprockets and tracks.
I thought: this is what poetry is,
although where my thought would head
after that, I wasn't exactly sure. At least
it was a thought, not some random memory
hung with the taffy of association
or an image dredged up from an image bank,
the private person's private store.
But the fact is, you grieve, and you
stare down the barrel of a cannon
at the same time, and you don't know why
there should be a connection,
or how you got in range of such a thing.
And then it happens again, as if

to say, *sic semper* to chance.
Yet something yokes them both
in the mind and, as Wallace Stevens
would have said, the mind of the poem.
I have often noticed it, and I know
that you must have too. Let the poem
teach, let it point a finger and declaim
as the highway unrolls seemingly forever,
in the face of grief and the barrel's mouth.
There was nowhere you could have arrived.
And the dark heart just sit there.

This Much I Can Tell You

for Jordan Smith

Sometimes it feels as if the mind
will seal itself up and you can go
a great distance without ever seeing
those who ever spoke your name.
You hear everything from cacophony
to a symphony played on instruments,
provenance unknown, stored out of sight
long ago. It's a closed system
but vast, and time unfolds there too,
unrelenting, nothing in abeyance,
like animal eyes suddenly appearing
in the roadside weeds and fields,
through which the highway plunges,
and on it a car traveling, not speeding,
not hanging back either. This much
I can tell you: there is smoke
beyond the mind, to which the mind turns,
as to a burning house, flames raging,
spurting from the second story windows.
Shouldn't you be running up the lawn?
Shouldn't there be, in truth, more fires?

'68

I was reminded of the Wallace rally
back in '68, the country music molding
the crowd, the police cordon complete
with billy clubs, my friends and I
in the rear, sarcastic and quiet, dissolving
our contempt in the dish of humor.
I've waited nearly 50 years to write this,
how we did nothing else, but hung back,
his "pointy-headed intellectuals," that
sunny day. It was like walking up
to the glass at an aquarium to see funny-
looking fish pausing and staring back,
each species regarding the other.
Wallace was right about us: when the police
shoved back we scattered. But the little man
didn't miss a beat, arms flailing, sometimes
windmilling, fanning the rhetoric. Our skulls
escaped, but fear never outweighed our
satisfaction. We repaired to a bar, smoked
Larks and drank loudly, as college students do,
pulling off impressions and quips. Where
are my comrades now? I don't even remember
who they were. I suppose it's time for apostrophes,
for some invocations to the forces beyond,
but that seems maudlin now, even pretentious.
I do remember my last glimpse of the man
as I was running. I could still see that
leering mouth that worked the crowd
into frightening self-righteousness: everything
had been stolen from them, and the time

had come to take it back. They didn't
even notice the commotion in the rear:
some hairy kids in need of correction.
There were fairground pennants too, rippling
onstage, the kind you see now at used-car lots.
I have traded in my memories for images.
But he was right: everything is stolen.
The highway tires do their work, pressing
down hard, until the road kill becomes a slick,
and predictably, without notice, the road again.
The ignorant have a right to be personally offended.
Even a racist country boy could see that.

Clothespins

In the end, Hegel says, it's all war.
But we're not at the end, are we?
We are somewhere along the spectrum
marking what was, like the way
my mother used to leave the clothespins
on the line at the very place she had
placed wet sheets, pants, towels, socks.
They were stories too, the clothespins,
though what they marked, in light
of early death and despair is hard to say.
And was there one for regret?
There should have been many for that
and the line long. I had thought if only
momentarily about Hegel because
I was also thinking about the power
of language to bring about love
in the face of the failure of language
to revive that same love. An old
professor, now deceased, once told me
that he had dreamt the last words
of Shakespeare, viz., "words are fleas."
He was a professor of drama,
of course. What other person
would have such a dream, both
demented and true? For if words
are true, Hegel is right, and the poem
that drew the lover in gave way
to the useless one that couldn't sing
her into staying. And yet, the fleas
get attention too, no doubt about that.

I will never forget a September Saturday
I went to a football game at LSU.
At halftime, the announcer barked
that former Governor Jimmie Davis
would lead us all in a song.
A tiny geriatric in a cowboy hat
mounted the endzone stage and stood
with his guitar before a mic.
He strummed and sang the first words.
Suddenly a hundred thousand fans
in that great bowl rose as if on cue
and began singing, "You are
my sunshine, my only sunshine…"
Everyone had the words, as they say,
by heart, and I too fell under the sway
of the mass enchantment, finding
myself having to deal with hot tears,
yet singing along in a choir of a hundred
thousand souls with the one-term,
one-hit governor from Lost Time
who had such sweetness, such sorrow—
a politician no less. As I say,
such sorrow, such collective sorrow,
marked in a song in the heart of everybody.

Armature

The building was immense and empty.
I hoped Bede was right and that sparrow
would find the skylight and fly
his crazy route from one emptiness
to another, like the swallows in Wal-Mart
that flicker and dart among the girders.

When Zeus showed up, I pointed out
this was my soul, abandoned
and cheapened by consolation.

But I found I was addressing the air,
arm extended in frozen emphasis
like the statue of Saddam Hussein
the elated mob toppled and jumped on
revealing its cheap, spinal armature,
before peace and the real war began.

The Takeaway

It was as if a small reckoning
had taken place because I
looked down and all I could see
was my napkin fallen like a sail
over the pontoons of my shoes,
pointing in your direction.
And when I raised my eyes
there were our plates and scraps,
a residual rim of sauce on one
like a distant coastline;
the other in similar disarray:
bones, tomato wheels lying by.
I averted my gaze, because I knew
yours was there, patient, waiting,
with that steadfast charity.
And that was the takeaway,
so I walked down the street
skirting the river, wind still warm
from the finished summer,
clouds starting to assemble.
Someone passed and I heard,
"I am of the opinion that..."
I crossed the street and stepped
down the subway stairs
like an Academy Award Winner
who knows to pause after such steps
before moving on to the transport
in the very place where the actual
stops, and the symbolic begins.

Falsetto

I saw Frankie Avalon and Lou Christie once
with their shirts off. It was outside, May,
Louisiana, their modest torsos QT-ed, each
wearing a Rolex the sun would catch
glinting, as they lifted the mic up delicately
to their Elvis-imitating mouths and belted
the fistful of fervid hits for which they
had formed the oldies revue aimed at ironists
and romantic questers like me. Why we
rose to stand there, the sweating congregation
of us, I can't say, except we were served
by mock enthusiasm, the *en-theo*, or God-in-us
we came away feeling. And not Avalon,
with his Hebe-like face and curled locks,
whose routine tenor rode a wave of melody
until it petered out like foam. It was Christie,
with that screechy larynx, as if fleeing fire,
who seemed suddenly yanked from earth.
He had discovered he had two faces,
and the shock of realization propelled him
upward, hair frozen, trunk sleek, defenseless
and boney. Yet he was suddenly striving toward God
because only He could rescue the Everyman
otherwise ensnared in banalities of the mortal coil,
not the least of which was the pressure of desire
and the subsequent covering up to restore
a semblance of equilibrium. But everyone knew
it was merely, in Salinger's phrase, sad-making.
It was not worth the saccharine, much less
a voice taking wing in an unnatural register

to arrive at the door of such a vapid mystery
as failure. It was as if the emotion's allegorical
figure stood before self-esteem long enough
to allow forgetting to melt it all away.
This is my theme: how a pop star poked
a hole in the sky and flew into it so that
heaven would know what we have always known:
that one face was not enough to be true.
When I understood that, I could have
laid my treasures at his feet, declared him
my King, except that he, Lou Christie,
was of course a knockoff and moreover headed
to the bin where records go, where they become
trash never to be recycled beyond a paltry
decade or two, so as to be closer to us,
as we are music to death itself, a ratio
pleasing no doubt to the Heaven of Plato,
endlessly soaring, high-pitched, and perfect.

Ten-Second Delay

That Blake etching, the angel hovering
over a skeleton, holding a trumpet.
At first, we were unable to hear its note,
or make out the skeleton stirring, at first
daintily, then the winching pull, accompanied
by sighs and the clicking of bones as it
sat upright. Nor could we see.
It's a surmise, which brings
me to her mouth, now talking
as our eyes locked across a small
chasm, her face against itself,
sprinkling confectioner's sugar atop
an ordinary, unassuming bread.
The food of love for the fools of love.
It's said TV cameras enforced
a ten-second delay so that
if Wallenda fell, the cameras could
cut away, and have nothing revealed,
although a body plunging through
space travels like the note
from the angel's instrument.
Therefore the Africans on Canal St.
pursue us with phrases, "Rolex! Rolex!
Vuitton! Vuitton!" the obviously fake
and shoddy goods pressed upon us
on every side in the voices of angels
in Blake, in the gauntlet of Blake.
The car horns mount up into a brass
section. The policeman, a conductor,
lets some through. Others must sing

if honking is song, their squalid
heartbreaking anthem, that fits my love
for the lost cause it must have been.
For each was armed with a tenderness
like an arctic creature melting into the wild,
truly long gone for the other, and from
the other, when dinner led us out
into the night, the ceaseless traffic,
where we parted, so filled and filling
with unspeakable acceptance
we hesitated, before the pattern
of divergence gave way to wind
and cold, first things without agenda,
which was loneliness as we felt it.

Empire Service

It seems to take longer than usual
for the train to emerge from the tunnel.
Broken buildings, then rocky banks
of the river and weedy masses rushing
past. At Tarrytown, the phone glows,
but it's not a real light, not a light
you can read by. Rather, it's your face.

I have lost the power to explain myself.

At Croton, a wedge of ducks
makes way across the still inlet.
Farther out, swans. Two of them.
Just for a second do they register.
Weeds are everywhere out there.
And yet it's winter and they're dead too,
though still standing at attention,
still presenting themselves somehow
to the vines, the trunks, the sky.
Then off in the distance I hear the horns,
warning of the train, and I'm on it.

Unfriend Me

I used to crank up a Toni Braxton song
when I drove through the Virginia
mountains at night on my way to a certain
studio on a hill. It was a dream. There I used
to find my zone at the end of my hand,
something personal, some small Rubicon,
like rotgut to a sot, a coded message,
and press Enter. I was a foot above the law,
a pelican among a scythe of pelicans
swooping over waves. Meantime,
I was this other person too, one who
winched words from the dark: liar,
prevaricator, poet whose catch, after
silent months, came up gleaming,
like creatures found next to a volcano
vent puckered on the seafloor. Soon
to be examined, named, prized for a while,
then put away. The way we do. The way
scientists do because they must get home.
So much is going on in the ordinary
there's no time to track specimens.
There are charts and labels ready to hand
for that. As for home, the man finds life
in trivial urgencies, the flotsam and small
change, housework, bills, dishes, whatever,
and later that night, as husband, drapes
his arm over his wife and covers her crotch
with his big, plain hand before the first dream
is even finished, and she, also dreaming,
covers his hand and tenderly pulls it away.

Composition

And then there was the Greek poet
who heard a man had died upstairs
in the boarding house where he was drinking.
He pleaded with the undertaker to delay
removing the body before he had a chance
to address it. So insistent was he that he
was granted his request and spent the night
reading poems over a dead man's body,
expecting a resurrection to rival Lazarus.
All night long he chanted his best work
and finally descended, haggard and dispirited.
It is the power of language that it doesn't
need to tell you how the story ends: it is
the crispness of pine, after the air of summer.

Helmets

Then there was Pavarotti singing,
"*Donna non vidi mai*" above the random talk
of bookish patrons. Like always,
I waited, a grown man, for the tears;
strangely they didn't come.
I am already on the other side,
I thought, that I can get the sign
and let it pass. Here, where
the paintings are so dark no light
can show what they depict, it was like
being wedged between Caravaggios,
except that there was no source of light.
Here I met the great poet frequently,
when I was the junior great poet,
but that was years ago.
We had espressos and ransacked the world
for the seeds of poems so as not
to be cut off like an unfinished sentence.
He died in his sleep, I am told.
Again with the Pavarotti, and still
no tears, still no signal and no light
on the field of the paintings.
But you can make out a pewter
helmet on one, and then another:
one tilted, one as if looking sideways.
Why were we not expecting this?
What kind of soldiers are we?

Infidel

One day I will find myself tired
of the unique and stylish dispatches,
the small news that hides the big:
a moment that passed in silence
by a brick wall, while in another place
a small moan, muffled by his body.
One day, the words will run out.
I will open the book, and they will
have left only the merest intimation
that they once stood like defenders
of the throne, the T's stiff as halberds,
the shield-like C, and the others.
One day there will be no reason to know
I held you up, as I had been taught,
by poets who thrived on impossible tasks
and while they were alive, boasted
to each other, competing for the most
outlandish claim, the one not to be
undone, the truth so steady that time
itself must withdraw, bowing.
But mostly it will be odd and doubtless
boring to have been of service so long,
contradicting the real and the obvious
like political advisers in a dictatorship,
like Mugabe reciting the little he knows
of T. S. Eliot and then the staffers applaud.

Miss Tilley

My friends went in fear of Miss Tilley,
as did I. And yet we were enjoined
by our young mothers and fathers
to take Latin, since it was "the key
to English" and all that lay beyond.
That steely partridge made cold calls
while we sat, wishing ourselves smaller
and smaller still, finally invisible,
parsing Caesar. *"Gallia est omnis divisa
in partes tres,"* droned the dictator.
"You can only parse verbs," she admonished,
"You can't parse a noun, much less
a sentence." Flushed out for humiliation,
one by one, we took pride in survival.
The T.W.I.U. had called out a strike,
and I followed my father as he paced,
placard in fist, past the smudge pots
lighting the factory's locked doors.
My mother stockpiled canned goods,
then filled boxes for the union hall.
The oily fires burned for days,
the black smoke sagging in air.
There was Belgium and Aquitaine.
And the third? That I forget: so what?
Men willingly believe what they wish,
as Caesar remarked later.
Miss Tilly died unmarried. I used
to pass her house, which seemed
as shut as a tucked-away jewel casket.
Who knows what might have been

stored there, as if put by, as if
looking out, so late, so long ago,
a great deal was on her mind?

Out of the Past

It would be in the evening
in front of the TV, you would
put your leg over mine.
And we would sit like that
with Anderson Cooper,
watching the world going
to hell, watching *The West Wing*.
The table before us held fruit
and nuts, cheese and olives.
A scene from a banal marriage,
perhaps, but that was
the magic of it: a whole year
in that house, with the suspicious
neighbors next door. Then *Laura*
and *Out of the Past,* and I would
take your foot and rub it.
Then the other, pressing the arch
carefully, working the muscular
tightness, the tough heel, ball,
and toes, bones and ligaments.
It had a rhythm like a song
wrapped around a refrain
in which all you ever meant
and all you desire are folded in
an artless verse. It was hand's
version of love songs composed
in a chamber by someone
remembering love, not living
in its company. But then, they
were feet being made ready.

When I held them they pointed
toward heaven. When I put them
down, they pointed away.

Dream Baby

A covey of burqas goes by the laundry,
travel agent, and bar; babies roll along,
concealed in layers in strollers.
Men clustered, the conversation,
whether sports or politics, serious.
Russians stare at the Greeks
and the Greeks stare back at the Russians,
no suspicion, no swapping talk, either.
It's the ultimate, isn't it?
How in this weather, the individual
man shears off from the collective,
and the collective must only wait
a short length to find him again,
that individual now coming up the block,
flushed, cap askew. Where was he?
Someplace where the shadow hesitated,
no doubt. Immigrants in eddies,
a buttery sunlight in a world of sorrow.
I have often thought I should turn from the world
to live in the poem, like the man in the tree
who pulls the ladder up after him,
as if to wed the anonymous and the personal
among the leaves, the clattering branches,
there in the wild perfection of the tree.
Or to stand suddenly among set pieces
and floor exercises, imagining how it will be
not to move, a squirrel on the forest floor
betraying presence with an uncontrollable flick,
while the spirit he remembers moves
by his immobile face in the form of a breeze.

Of my bona fides let it be said,
it was only the life I wouldn't possess,
or that wouldn't own me, that was
my text. Now I forage for the key:
the square or the round? I forget.
Like an acorn or a booster falling away,
even the Beloved, who in my dreams
made care a spotted fruit and death
a feather: reduced to a period.
A man raps inaudibly on the door.
The light in the upstairs window
is small, but it covers everything.

As If

It's said that the sentence, "I am alone"
is a contradiction, since utterance
all by itself implies a recipient
and hence the presence of another, intended
or real. Ironically, it's such rationalizing
that leads to loneliness in the first place
for aloneness is unremarkable, if
not unremarked. I watched a yellow,
violin-shaped patch of sunlight today
on the wall and waited to see if slow time
would allow me to observe light's creep.
Then a stratus cloud over my shoulder,
backed up by the upstate winter sky,
abruptly cancelled the test with the finality
of Michelangelo who is said to have
critiqued a beseeching pupil's sculpture
by slamming it into a wall.
My new study was bare, except for a desk,
unpainted, and three unmatched chairs.
There were plenty of windows,
as if to say to the loneliness: come,
let the day itself, so full of time, absorb you,
exchanging *seem* for *seen*, *lonely* for *alone*,
with no loose ends, no toxic byproduct.
But the *Inferno* tells a different story,
how in the harrowing the granite split
and the mine was suddenly in danger
of catastrophic collapse, a menacing silt
streaming from the cracks and seams,
not to mention the demons with iron gaffs,

charcoal monkeys and their obscenities.
It would have been the destruction of hell.
The real battle was with the poet's words,
which were the weapons of choice,
hived in clichés, stuttering with imprecision,
until having secured the puzzled hostages,
the unspoken hero led them back through
the very cracks and still-smoking holes
that were the result of the intrusion,
the red-hot inches and dark discriminations.
Even as a rumor, it was what it was,
keeping just one step ahead of the devil,
as my grandmother used to say,
bending the note until it was almost a question,
before turning back to the sink.

On a Line from CK

Those days of the snow, of wincing at
the bright window as if not only distance
but time itself might appear, and not its effects.
For that moment only, I keep the days
in their own recess in memory's theater.
And the processional flow of the Hudson
when you were not there. And yet
I hugged sorrow as if it were joy.
It was sorrow. The world was tipping
like a boy I pulled from the balcony rail
once in Dublin, so drunk he was delirious
and never felt the hands that yanked him
back into life. For that moment only,
he was free. And I was pulled back
though I knew the hands that took me,
the arms when I came to rest, the face
near mine, the sweet, improbable smell.
Those days when I only waited for time
to mill its grain through me, never seeing
how that same time hastened to rescue me.
Until one night, at the peak of love
she bit my face hard and drew blood
and then fell back like Eurydice
into the dark pillows without a cry,
before and after rushing to the border
for that moment only, separating us.

Stay

When we had walked the length of Warren Street,
my daughter asked me, in the sweetly
patronizing way of clever girls, how old
Maurice Williams had been when he
and The Zodiacs recorded the classic
two-minute position-paper on longing:
"Stay," complete with its own wish-
fulfillment charm: "Say that you will."
I said he must have been in his twenties,
the decade that aligns artifice
with sincerity, after which it's a chore
to sustain any falsetto lament.
At the same time, I pointed out, he was
all over YouTube warbling his hit,
Bogarting the mic like every one-hit wonder,
through the non-sequitur decades,
to bobbing Bandstand teens, variety shows,
and of course, soul revivals, and he
could be seen there at different ages,
the question of high notes notwithstanding.
O Stay! Thou art so fair, cried Faust to Helen,
in translation. We were about to board
a train that follows the river into the city,
where the announcement would take place,
the day finally at hand. The Hudson,
frozen in misty, extruded chunks,
was like an executive takedown of the gentle
ticking of the ice flow in Lowell's poem,
whose puzzle-piece blanks seemed
to bear some mystery beneath, some image,

instead of what they really were—
pate-gray on either side, with no figure
to reassemble, either in the mind of God
or in the passage—parade, really—
by the sense-making city. In other words,
it was hard, dazzlingly crisp, dead-
brilliant with the hush of the north.
Houses balanced on ledges and banks,
later along the flaky Palisades like redoubts
of some cold war unrecorded, but not therefore
unexperienced. People died out there
as the river, so the hymn tells us, bore them,
although it seemed a solid floor too. I
thought how the long street down to the river
seemed with their shops and houses
to bear our recent impression, the seal
of a common life, now hooked into its drift,
content to board. For a moment I thought back
to the summer before, when we had strolled
down it, hand in hand, determined to resist
and be, momentarily, so far from the water.

The Red Dot

After we embraced at the crosswalk
in the coarse fidelity of separation
our chests together one brief last time

in the rain, in the bluster, the puddles,
the honking taxis, the herds of umbrellas,
then my family rose from their silos

and crossed the sky to find me.
My mother and father like a flying
boxcar, my father with his trumpet,

then my brother with the hole
in his temple untouched, soaring
up the east coast, practically

stratospheric, like a hawk in autumn,
whose vision increases with distance,
looking to find me, past the forests

of Pennsylvania, past the Pine Barrens,
finally turning east before Paterson,
down through swirling pipes of rain,

the dark copper clouds, the towers
rising from the river, the shining rooftops,
my mother and father swerving out,

then turning in from the sea, looking
to land, looking for their other son,
the one who had summoned them

and my brother whose eternal muteness
would someday become speech,
and that pass for eloquence, as

Nietzsche himself reassured us. I came
home and sat by the computer screen
checking, as I had always done,

for the ruby dot announcing a message,
light that burns a hole in everything,
a change of heart as if the heart were

no longer hurtling into the rain, no longer
losing, anxiously whispering, *change me.*
Instead, I heard them overhead.

I looked up and we smiled at each other.
I was being airlifted by beloved
spirits called to the old vastness

from the sleep of their cylinders,
who bore my name, who still believed,
sleepy as they were, that they knew me.

Up we went and I saw Canal shrink
into a line, the line into a spinning
propeller, so I looked straight up, my family

pulling me up in the updraft, through
the plunging temperatures, until it was
full black, and yet there were stars.

Here they peeled off and faded,
leaving me; they were just clouds
themselves now, morphing and turning.

Because I was vexed, I pretended
it was them. Because there was no
red dot, only black city rain,

I found myself floating, knowing
how Pluto would rise from his throne
pointing earthward, not heavenward,

though I was exalted in my wedding suit
waiting to have my ears rubbed,
which was the special sign for love

for no one could mistake thinking
that's what it's like. Not even
the sweet dead in their cerements.

Not even a stranger.

The Porch

The upper porch is rickety and could come loose
at any time. A black mud dauber
lands on a square of sunlight, rotates
for a moment on a two-by-four, then is gone.
Nervous sleep and day demanding: diesels
hum between some trees and the hot sky,
which has dismissed any chatter of clouds.
An old gray cat, like the past, drags its long tail
through the gravel. Shadows move across the siding
like Plato's cave where he sits, perched. Without being
there, he knows what the river is doing:
it's the same thing that marks the appearance
of the creatures: groundhog, skunk, a nearly invisible fawn
he spotted between the woods and the road
when he came down the mountain, seeds wandering, falling
like cotton from the tall trees. They were en route
happy enough to be blind in the landing, just as the trees
shook them off indifferently. He could draw
the lesson, but in his singularity, does not.
Better to end on the images, as the poet said, let them form
from the void, take whatever shape is theirs
and like the old masters of figure and ground, go from that.

The King of Thebes

There were the barefoot girls in see-through dresses,
and she had been one of them. She pauses to let that
sink in. Just then a house wren flies up to the window,
looks in curiously and darts out of the frame.
He knew them too, so many summers back, so many
towns-with-a-square ago. His were different beaches,
some with bunkers that spoke of an even older time,
all with the rippling sea grass, as if people leaned
against a cordon, waving to their favorite movie stars
who stepped from limousines, faultless in tuxedos
and furs, and made their way to the premiere.
She speaks in a low, conclusive voice across the table,
opens a fresh pack of cigarettes and selects one
from the back row of the pack, like a magician
choosing a helper from the back of the nightclub.
There are no more birds now, and the window frames
her head, the new hair not as glamorous as the old.
Then there is the whisky, which has been sitting on the floor
by her chair, named after a man, himself silhouetted
on the label. She speaks of the first husband, now dead,
how he had squirreled away boxes of porn, even
as he descended into Hades with his memory wronged
by the ghouls sent to pick through his remains.
Pity rises in his mind, though he knows it doesn't belong there.
She pushes the cigarette pack in his direction,
but he only remembers, for a moment, his father hunched
and terminal, and then all those other men
who fought so bravely when the war crashed ashore.
They are small figures now, punctuation marks that guide
the mind across its terrain. He knows the girls

on her beach; they too wish to be accorded a name,
but he can't come up with any. He may have slept with a few
once, but birdsong leaves everything winsome and vague.
She means to say there is greatness abounding
in small amounts, blowing smoke that the screen catches
and directs outside. His pity is abstract to her,
like a ceremony where presence is a placeholder, when men
in suits stand silently by women in dark gowns,
having discharged the obligations of the outside
to the inner force that drives the bridegroom to unite
with the sailor. But she is a friend to such sacrifices,
and she deserves the bottle at her foot, the whisky
she sips from a cup, as though it were the King of Thebes
who offered up a toast, lest the war be forgotten,
lest it be turned over to the bird, still audible
above the angry traffic, the horns, and the jackhammer.

A Breakfast

Daddy is fixing breakfast this morning:
country ham, fried eggs, grits and red-eye.
He calls it "breakfast of champions."
My mother is pinning the wash to the line.
I can see her through the window, bending
to the basket, standing up, an assembly line.
I'm embarrassed at the row of underwear,
but why? The neighbors have their lines.
An earwig pops out and wiggles across the sill.
Then my brother emerges, stands sullen
in the doorway, before sitting at his place.
Not much to say, and yet so much unsaid,
so much we bring to the table, its thin
white tablecloth that touches our knees
as we sit. Before long, we will all be
heading out, under the crop of our masters.
But not this morning: time has no business here.
What the mockingbird can't see, as it
perches flickering in the bush, neither
will it sing, as the day brightens.
Neither will I sink to interpretation,
who sing, and forfeit the dead.

The Earwig

The way chance spaced the trees
gives the eye a runway to the black point
just before the turnpike, itself
invisible, until the leaves burn
and finish. If I had a soul—
and who's to say I can't sing
in these terms?—that's where
I would find it, that dark spot
looking back at me, if, that is,
it could look back through
the young trees to the old
and the dead still rising on the bank
of the brook, as if they too had
a purpose and stood as tall
as the sky allowed. But I am here,
where an earwig, paused on the slate,
stirs and begins making its way
across the flecked, moving surface,
as if in dance, but there is no dance,
just yes and no in sequential volley,
rendered by leaf-shade and sunlight,
just as Hopkins described it
a hundred and fifty years ago,
only minus belief, just crawling,
nothing simpler, on its way to the soil.

Not the Mighty but the Weak

It was in a library, or, what passed for a library
in an old house on the leeward side of a hill.
He could not hear the ocean, but it was there,
over the other hills, and sent clouds scudding
far inland. The leaves, furious, were falling.
He thought to blow them over the edge
so as to build the hill. There had been a stone
wall that went down to the stream, but it had
collapsed under some regime no one remembers.
There was Emerson, of course, and Pierce
and certain other madmen whose souls
reverberated in the silence of the books:
buckram and board, jaundiced paper, glue and thread.
He knew the condition and pitch of each soul,
but not of his own, for his life had spread,
extending first forward, then through memory.
But now it had mysteriously circled back upon itself.
Death was spreading through him now
because death was jealous of the intricate tracery
his life had arrogated to itself. But death's decline?
Death's *own* dying? That was the thing.
The comity of the dead, for whom
he had scant breath. Yet he was custodian.
Then Emerson said, "Do not mistake the thunder
for the verse. The incomprehensible poem
is the truest." He also said other things,
or so the custodian thought, but mostly
it was the unremitting fury of the leaves,
the yawing of the shelves where he paced,
and sheets of dust. All the same, the house

stood, and the clouds crossed over in ranks,
their shadows through the window
passing over the stacks whose spines
darkened momentarily. The stream felt
them too, and took them briefly in
before taking them altogether, as if
completion was a subject fit for a library
whose freshest word murmured anxiously,
on and on, from an impossible distance.

from
School of the Americas
(2012)

Shum

I went with my teacher to a lecture once
in an ornate hall: long windows and Empire chairs.
The diminutive scholar was legendary:
he had been a confidante of Mayakovsky
and friend of the then-still-living Lilya Brik.
He had made formalism all the rage and so
blended nicely at Harvard when Stalin yanked
the choke-chain, and poets vanished in
binges of murder, imprisonment, and suicide.
We were late, and only a few unoccupied seats
were scattered about the hall. So down
the aisle we strode past more professors
than I had ever seen in one place.
Bearded, severe, they followed our entrance
with all the disapproval a Ph.D. can muster.
My teacher, a fierce blonde and former model,
bore herself with the halo of two well-received books
and parked herself on the front row, me next to her.
This distinguished professor announced that he
would recite a poem by Velimir Khlebnikov
by way of warming to his subject,
which was "sound verse," in Russian—*shum*.
Then he began to present what Khlebnikov
had claimed was a new poetry to counter
the tyranny of significance. Stepping gingerly
before the august audience, he started
to emit clicking sounds and to gesture
like an old-school Thespian. A silence went up
from the audience, unsure if it was
being played, or if it was just collectively

missing the boat altogether. At that point
my teacher reached into her purse
and extracted a compact and brush.
She opened the compact and gazed
at her own countenance for what seemed
a full minute, then began to brush
her hair with long strokes, pausing
every few to extract the captive hairs
and drop them on the university carpet.
The scholar pretended there was nothing
amiss and soldiered on with his rendering
of the poet's cricket impression, nonetheless
aware of the Amazonian woman not four
feet from him, so tall that in merely sitting
she easily matched his standing height.
When she had done, she put the brush away,
checked herself one last time, then snapped
the compact shut. With hands in lap
she sighed once and turned to the poetry reading
at last, letting her gray eyes come to rest
on the important little man and his recitation.
To this day, I don't know which was the better
performance. But each taught me something invaluable
about poetry, that art where I stood eager
to begin my work, that small country,
that Switzerland of decorum and peace
that lies between nonsense and vanity.

Canoe

Well into September the gardenias
were squeezing out their heavy smell
deep from the sugar of rot and pre-rot.
It was like Canoe, the cheap cologne
boys used to slap on their cheeks
before they went forth to meet the girls
who would pick over them (on this account)
and leave many in the emotional disarray
of having been passed over. But for some,
it was the smell of victory and reward,
and those grew sweet and strong, even
mythic, in the belief that nature,
or at any rate, their lives, possessed
a coherence that they could access
with their smooth skin, muscles,
and good teeth. No one suspected
any collusion with death, and only those
whom Giuseppe Belli called the "dog faces"
caught the faint decay that streamed after
the chosen swirled by, and even these
failed to draw any but a fair conclusion
because the moon was like that,
streaming over the lawn, and the music,
although the words were inane,
pierced lovers and failures alike
with its silver needle moving in and out
of a fabric they don't make anymore.

In Passing

The artist I once compared to Ulysses
who learned to chisel frowns from quarried stone,
who painted ugliness like an angel
when the art world turned from the god-hunters,
high on infinity, in favor of the urban cool
of joke and technique, died an artist's death
on the throne, midday, disappearing from
the nurse's eye into the silence of marble.

Our last visit, he emerged, gloved and rubber-
aproned, pushing his jeweler's visor bought
to disarm glaucoma, up over still-thick hair,
pausing only to point the walker more narrowly
down the ramp to his sitting room.
From there, he commenced the last lesson:
space, contour, line, stepping forth into it.
He had lost none of the manic zeal with which

years earlier he cajoled Matta into buying
a used helicopter and brought from Italy
a Roman beauty, formerly a model, and had her
dream self-creation so deep she slashed
canvas after canvas, until he showed her
how to find the ledge where space took off
and craft fell backward like a discarded barrel,
the space of the painting, I mean.

You're better than Schnabel! he thundered
at my wife, who, like a soul in Dante,
saw already the dead memory overlaid
on the old man sitting at her elbow.
She had come with her portfolio,
the student now grown powerful herself.
He urged her to study *The Last Judgment*
that ultimate in large-scale organization.

Look at Kline, he said, *though he doesn't
go far enough.* Always the plane: *how
many dimensions to the plane?* He hurried
to answer his own question. *Depth is not
optical,* he said, *and empty depth is not
space. When things are nebulous you have
to affirm the negative with clear images.
The deeper it goes the flatter it gets.*

The negative decides the contour. Hours
of this. Weeks later, I wonder how all
the cicadas draw down their racket,
then send it spinning back through the trees,
leaving dusk to sound, night to insight
because the negative space has to be positive.
And because it is evening back at the stone,
a small plane passing joins the mower.

North State

My father came to me in a dream
to walk with me around a stadium.
Not wearing the jaunty motley of his last months:
the patchwork newsboy cap and paneled shirt
he wore when tearing around town,
smoke streaming from the car window.
"I'm not gonna make it," he said.
"This may be the last time.
I don't have the breath for it."
We cried and smiled all at once.
The apparition faded, and I lapped the spot
before I knew. That morning
I had stopped to take some pictures
of a new structure: a five-story globe
affixed to a museum headquarters.
It was Sunday, the crews were gone,
but the wooden scaffolding clung
to the girders, "North State Steel"
spray-painted on each rib.
I had come before the planks were taken away
like cross-hatching erased,
before the world was made,
the panels bolted in place and painted
that planetary blue of earth from space,
that pendant marble
on which everything is always lost
like a glass eye that never sees
what it never ceases to watch.

The Stegosaurus

His name was Butch, and I was his bitch,
that is, me, Mikey, Randy, Charles
and Kenny were, rounding out a handful
of chumps who came home through the woods
where he lay in wait and gestured us to understand
we were pussies until, the attitude escalating,
he punched us out with hickory-hard fists,
saliva flying from his hissing mouth.
He had fled the School for the Deaf
and hitched three hours to Durham
though he was unable to utter a single word,
signing and grunting until his intimidated rides
deposited him on his family's street,
which was our street. He never returned
to signing school, never learned a trade
but sat in a Barcalounger until he was forty,
and his parents had become ancient courtiers,
the only ones who intuited the wishes
of the lizard-lidded Nordic giant.
Company came and went, including myself,
and he would greet me by jerking
his head back a notch in a knowing way,
and let his eyes hold onto mine for a full second.
That was it: the peerless, punishing friend
of my youth lost in his boredom but sending
the ping of a message from the past
like a trapped collier who needed no skill
to show that silence and sounds compete
for the same stone, the one Yeats placed
in the middle of his great poem.

He pummeled the shit out of me one day,
while I was carrying my first library book,
a boy's story about a stegosaurus.
I managed to twist around and get him
in a headlock; nor would I release him
until his body conceded, and we lay panting
on either side of the path. That day
he acknowledged me by holding before me
his fist, which he then thrust into his pocket,
before departing. That day too I buried the novel
about the stegosaurus—I don't know why—
and made a note of forgetting anything
that happened to me until such time
as it made sense—me with words,
Butch with his massive arms menacing
the school path. It was late '62,
Kennedy and all just down the other road
and on their way into our new lives.

Charlotte Mew

Something emerged from motes
the late afternoon sun had set spinning
inside a golden shaft. It was a lightning
bug too immature for the beacon
to have formed out the back of him.
Like a cursive "W" it made its way
looping across the space dividing
the nearer nothing from the farther.
I had been reading Charlotte Mew.
I was searching for a cadence of hers
that reemerged from the throat
of an older male poet some years back,
when I had sat in on his workshop
despite the obvious creeping dotage,
just to hear stories and recitations.
Even at 86, he insisted on announcing,
in the alumni newsletter, every review,
every newly accepted poem, though
everyone already bowed to his eminence.
Not finding what I was looking for,
I thought it could have been
just my mistake. Such a loss
is not unlike a wind chime's
unrepeatable melody or someone's
aping a language they don't know.
You need the words, whatever else
bears witness to the dance in middle air.

The Hook

It was during the opening bars
of Neil Diamond's "Sweet Caroline"
when he sings, "I can't begin to know when'"
that I first realized the value of my education.
All those poems and novels were not
just there to be appreciated and added
to the store of vicarious emotions.
They were there to make someone
see what an ass could emerge from
the loins of self-creation, when
an otherwise intelligent man sought
to escape his hackneyed feelings
by torturing English grammar just before
the hook that would propel him
one summer into pop superstardom,
before the slide into camp
and weary self-parody. That summer
I was about to be married, when a girl
named, in fact, Caroline, began flirting
with me at work. She was nineteen,
a brunette, and I would come home
from work both exhilarated and confused,
for the first time feeling how the push-
pull of ambivalence might not resolve
itself in commitment predicated on loss
but be a destiny all by itself, a fate
of coming down squarely on both sides.
Reader, I married her—not sweet Caroline
but my fiancée. We saw Neil Diamond
perform the following spring attired

in reptilian leather, shining and corrugated.
My new wife and I were far beyond
any sincere interest in such a sellout,
but for a Saturday afternoon outdoor concert,
it worked. A shower came up. Neil's skin
looked even more uncomfortable, but
showman that he was, he didn't betray
the mission. We covered ourselves
in a blanket, and the small cloud passed.
That night, I watched another show—
my body stippled in hideous hives—
the result of some allergen in the wool.
A few years later, graduated
and separated, I was driving in late summer
through western New York when I saw
Tesla's arcs, my first aurora, as startling
as hives. Sickles of light swept the sky
like a windshield wiper over the plains.
It must have lasted an hour. It had
come unannounced and unexpected, eerie,
but by then I knew exactly what it was.

Field Service Report

Herbert wrote it was like "sweets
compacted"—about a day like this.
May morning, little beings flitting
among weeds, songbirds refusing
to let traffic overwhelm their call-
and-response. I saw them coming:
Jehovah's Witnesses, two women
in long print dresses and two men
in black suits and black, wide-brimmed hats.
The women approached first, knocking
at the neighbor's door, the men
waiting on the sidewalk as if ready
to swoop in and shore up their efforts.
But there was no one at home.
I was sitting on the porch reading Cavafy
("Try to keep them, poet, / those
erotic visions of yours"). In my mind
I had been transported to a little town
in upstate New York, where years ago
I lived rashly but deeply, full of
youthful longing, according to the time.
But seeing this formal quartet circle back
on my block, I closed the book
on Cavafy's vision and my own
and went inside. There I let the breakfast
dishes clatter and the radio music wail.
I didn't want to hear the doorbell
with its peremptory summons.
I couldn't bear to see the tired,
angelic faces at my door, arms
full of literature, such was my anger.

Gil's Sentence

"Gil Scott-Heron to Be Sentenced"
—*NY Times*, July 9, 2006

"I find that rhetoric does my thinking for me,"
she said, turning the page, moving on,
having out-Plathed Plath, including
the bitchy conjurations of voice
that threatened to make all a trick
and fostered ill will. Next up, me.
I read my serious, inadequate verse,
remembering all the while the assassinating
queries of my undergraduate workshops:
"What is the function of the ego in this poem?"
"What does the third person mediate? Or is it
really you?" So often the poem came down
to *you*, and after my soft-voiced rendition,
silence followed suit, a reset button
before the class critic trained an interrogating
eye on one offending line. Elliott Coleman,
too aged and amiable to rein in
the revolutionary spirits of the seminar
pretended a real point of craft was at issue
and let the *sans-culottes* have their way.
"It's sentimental," said one. "The subject
is unstable," said another. I had
no answer to these indictments and sat
silently, a you, while the rest of the eyes
wobbled back and forth as if not quite
believing their luck in having stumbled
on a massacre. Then a large black man rose,
I mean actually stood up and in doing so

tipped over his unlocked briefcase
spilling old cups, record albums, a copy
of his recent (published) novel and some spoons.
Scanning the table, he who had been silent
all semester debuted a serrated baritone
that wondered about the merit of intention,
something he thought neglected. ("Intention is
the moon I follow," I seem to remember
his saying, though the verbatim is unsure.)
He was risen to that defense when justice
was poetic and of course snubbed me
later when I tried to ingratiate myself
with a little joke in our apartment elevator.
That other was about language: that was all.
But this was the weekend. He was in his
other world with his band, his other means.
Four or five menacing afros with shades
followed him silently up to a different view
of that white moon out in the alley,
beyond my place, beyond where I got off.

Redcaps

In the poem a camp survivor
explained that while a certain poet
I happen to esteem believed
that at the end of the road
a Word existed to explain it all,
 he, the survivor, offered instead the idea
that a silence, explaining nothing
was more worthy of a man of the world,
and implied the poet
was naïve to hold to his song.
I see it's a version
of what Kafka said: in the end
there's nothing ironic. No irony.
Think of it, reader! Therefore,
 you're no longer able to write of that
region where the word stops,
but something lies still ahead,
be it God or death, or just the thing,
whatever it is, beyond the best thought.
You have only bread or tea or oranges
in a bowl, and even that drags
its privilege like an old steamer trunk
the redcaps rush to fuss over so that you
can look around, and regard the dappling
as more than shade, while they push
the weight onto the wagon.

Roy Orbison, New Orleans, 1984

They were micro-operas, and he
was as lifeless a tenor, as could be
propped on a stage, so hidden in black
he seemed the emissary of oblivion,
except that there was nothing
he was capable of forgetting, no hurt.
He sang of disappointment straight up;
three blondes swayed to his catatonia.
I had separated from my wife
and appeared with my new interest,
a bi-polar space invader, as the years
would prove. On this lawn of denim
and tank-tops, we too moved
with the music. For Roy,
all of life's fullness survived only
in dreams, and because they did so
they were invariably sad, insubstantial—
yet within those boundaries, vivid.
Some years later I heard a fellow
read a paper at a conference.
His thesis was that Roy projected
a *posthumous* persona: the immobile,
obsidian figure drawing audiences
to that quavering falsetto, a voice
from beyond the grave, as warbly
as the gibbering, bloodthirsty ghosts
in Virgil. I mean, it was clever,
and I've thought of his point often.
Who doesn't wish, in some sense,
to talk back at experience

from the perspective of the concluded self?
It is a voice devoutly to be wished
that to the hearer would be a haunting;
to the singer, proof positive.
My ex-wife remarried, and to her
I am just a short that spun its way out
before the ponderous feature starring
a regular guy. My girlfriend got help,
but not before the worst
had befallen us, not before we said
what no earthings could take back.
At the next stage, the lead singer
had just taken his foot off
the wah-wah pedal like a driver
leaving the accelerator before applying
the brakes. Where did they think
they were going, the show-stoppers,
when the show was not in this life,
as we had just heard, and believed?

Get It Down

I had a friend who was so pathologically shy
he barely functioned in public. He was
in essence, a hermit living in a dune shack.
Unfortunately, he wrote poetry, and this
brought him to the attention of an art colony
that offered him safe haven, in return
for which he had only to push paper,
arrange chairs, and host weekly readings
by prominent poets. It was almost schtick
as he stood, a large man, before the gathering,
hands folded defensively over his crotch
and paused long enough to give
the audience, also, pause too before he swept
one hand mechanically, by way of introduction,
and blurted, "Miss Bishop!" or "Stanley Kunitz!"
then found his chair. It was a performance
of the highest order, in one sense,
and no one who was there ever forgot it.
He was a beautiful and mysterious poet too.
I said "unfortunately," only in the sense
that he had to overcome his shyness,
in order to look a fool in the eyes
of all. And I imagine him each time
going home from the weekly humiliation
to write the most radiant poems
as the green sea gnawed its way up
to the shack and the crabs scissored
across the wooden steps, as irrepressible
as I imagine Ritsos was, confessing
to his young executor, "You see, I'm
trying to get all this down before I die.

Mink

"Time can render true what began in falsehood."
—David Downie

We passed on Mink DeVille and went down
to another club where studded, junkie coxcombs
leaned against old brick, profiled Mohawks
like halos in Fra Angelico, at maximum extension.
We bumped and snorted, then met the dawn
glazed with dew, under the bridge, immortal.

Last night, I lay awake listening
to summer's revelers hooting drunkenly,
occasionally rising to fisticuffs—until light
crawled across the ceiling. Then, following
a moratorium hour, came the sound
of street cleaners scrubbing stone.

My own mother demonstrated how gasps
displaced breath until entropic muscle
ironed a vanishing point's V into a flat-line.
A poet friend gave my old inamorata
six to seven years to live, max. I saw us
staggering around the Village, brains ablaze,

swearing to hold our last meeting
in the same grave. Or so she said in a bar.
Those words, privileged, defiant, false,
words also spaced themselves from previous
until they fell silent—between us, I mean.
We met in a grave of words

but my fantasy kept a conversation
going about high and distant things.
That conversation gave shape to the eruption
of drunks bellowing on the pavement below
as they waited for the sweepers and the first
men in suits headed for the subway.

At the same time that spirit's rendition
of sweet nothings slobbered into the ear of a god,
I moved at the heart of a deep reverie.
The times between being all ordinary saviors
needed to hail souls to 2.0, I couldn't help
noticing the smell of water on stone

and thought of Auden's face, the penitent
carved from the young man, the way a teardrop,
advancing from its source, stains the almanac.

Talking Points

Reading the autobiography of her
ex-husband, my now-distant friend choked
with sarcasm at the omission of herself
and the children, seeing that as conclusive
evidence of a man, not self-promoting,
but self-erased. During the dinner
at which he had proposed more than
seventy years ago, he kept a cheat sheet
of talking points underneath his napkin
in case the conversation lagged. Thus no
one was surprised when, at his death,
he had left nothing of his estate
to his forbearing survivors, but divided
the dragon's hoard between the library
and parks, and his late-life, buxom
caretaker spouse. It was pure Groucho
in the obviousness of it, but disbelief,
like belief, boils the frog slowly. At the end,
his sixty-year-old children still craved
love's table crumbs, but he who had made
of himself the exception was scarcely
inconvenienced by his own demise.
Surrounded by the attentions of children
still starving for a nod or a touch, he
waved them away to stare at the sea
where he experienced a warm, valedictory fog,
his body released in its brittle turn, showing,
how even at the brink, one could be both
immersed in the wretched longings of others
and blessedly devoid of empathy too.

Russians

It wasn't the end when
my girlfriend handed me the phone
in the middle of the night and said,
"Here, say hello to my husband."
And it wasn't the end of anything
when another grabbed the wheel at 70
and screamed, "I could pull this
right off the road right now!
I could do it *right now!*"
Those frenzies have passed
into something like the memory
of a good novel, weighted in one's lap
when the day is cleared,
and there's nothing left to do
but look in on the Russians
passing out at the feet of their superiors,
emptying their wallets into the fireplace,
throwing their brain-stuffed heads
before the locomotive of History,
rather than face the vivid memory
of errors committed when the face
was hot and stared into the eyes
of that intransigent, that other face.

I Am Nobody

Behind the blue house rise
two massive oaks still in baby green,
their trunks like petrified aortas.
Elsewhere the darker green of summer
takes hold. But for now what's most
at issue is drifting across
the still bright sky at sundown,
clouds showing their undersides
like mating animals. For what thing
doesn't desire appraisal? Even
the blue, famously indifferent
to characterization of any sort
makes a habit of being watched
by forest eyes, wary of night
more than the head who thought,
"I am nobody," as it leaned to the barrel
that day, a day that fell backward
like a vending machine off a cliff,
the whole damned thing styled
for impact, that from the rim above
seemed silent and tiny, barely a puff.

The Assassination of Sadat

I was probably the last in my group
to drop acid. I did this the day
Sadat and Begin shook hands and stood
grimly cheerful before assembled dignitaries
and press. Between that day and Sadat's murder,
I rode a black motorcycle to work,
my tiny, perfect wife perched on back,
reaching her model's hands around
my middle—a garland of her arms:
the bride I would lose with one
careless affirmative on a day
no calendar saw coming. Instant replays
were the thing then, and we saw it
over and over, how the assassins rose
from the reviewer's stand and took down
the President in a bloody, chaotic shower,
then sat down again, hiding the automatic weapons,
as Sadat and company walked backwards
over to the chairs un-overturning,
to the hero's greeting, then a moment's rest.
Before he was gunned down again
and the '80s proved the arrow of time
as willful as any bullet. The black bike
I rode I bought cheap off a guy
after an accident involving his knee
and hot, colliding steel. The insurance
made the bike, unlike the knee, good as new.
It was a time when I rode safe,
knowing nothing of anything worth a life,

knowing only that, after truing, the tires
followed the road on their own.
Which was, you might say, the last thing
I needed to know, a guy like me.

At the Grave of Jesse Helms

The siren travelling from one side of the city
to the other is like that trick
of stereo separation in the old
Moody Blues song about Timothy Leary.
Playing with your head: the bouncing
sound ball traversing the terrain
between your ears, cupped in phones.
He was probably right to hate us.
I saw the bullwhip handle jammed
in that guy's anus and knew,
in the larger sense, you could
lay the fault at my doorstep.
Of the nuclear family, Flaubert
conceded, you know they're *right*.
These days I see the campaign photo
of Mitt Romney, his wife and kids
smiling calmly at the voter. They know
which burdens styled whiteness eases.
They have no use for old tactics—
let the pornographers stamp them
with the imprimatur of kitsch. Let
the bullwhip protrude from the black
man's ass: there's no art in the fetish.
Once my dad took me to an orphanage
to shake hands with Aunt Bea
from *The Andy Griffith Show*.
Aunt Bea was indisposed; in her place
stood Senator Helms, greeting Shriners
with a snaggle-toothed smile and courtly way.
I reached up and took the hand that made

Gorbachev tremble. I tremble myself now,
and yet, who's to wonder at what
the imagination has to do—to say nothing
of the world we hoped to shape
with it. That was a long ago, but not
even death has moved the issues along.
The heart is still with Mapplethorpe,
the man superimposed on the boy and
pausing, before he steps into the leather shop.

Masha

I'm listening to the violins shimmer,
a cheap and self-conscious attempt at
emotional presentiment, like Wordsworth's
daffodils, only black. It's perhaps only
a composer's joke (here, Rachmaninoff's)
so heavily does the music heave between
the quotation marks of what it feels, of what
in some way it must be, until it reaches
a chromatic delta, then regroups into
a swell of melody. To tell you the truth,
it reminded me—in the multivalent way
music does—of a time I drove to Montreal
to marry a Russian girl, Masha, so that,
like Auden's wife, she could peel off
immediately on crossing the border
and go her way into civilization, as Wystan
and Thomas Mann intended. I had been
put up to this escapade by a friend,
himself an émigré, and imagined its potential
far into the future, for literary treatment.
But what I found was a series of quizzical
beings, a mother, a sullen ex-husband,
and some other persons identifiable only
by grunts and movements in the background.
When Masha appeared, I beheld a woman
with a light but full mustache, a beauty
marred in an atrocious and pitiless way
not only by brutal politics, but
by something more hostile in nature,
something against which the mere

barbarities of the materialist State were
just buffetings of the otherwise inert.
We went for tea, and after listening to my
rehearsed entreaty, she told me in tenderness
and with tact, why this was a fool's errand,
why Canada, even with an ex-spouse in tow,
ended her pilgrimage more appropriately
than the States. I left as the sun eased
into the lake, feeling empty and ashamed
of using and also, of being used. I felt
like an aide-de-camp who had screwed up
at Yalta, having lost nuance and substance both,
and the second-to-last thing he remembered was
the swishing capes and the wheelchair's crunch,
as the principals exited the raised dais,
and everyone turned and glimpsed the Black Sea,
all swells and wheeling seagulls, one last time.

Sodomites

So he's standing there on the porch
telling me how the Tea Party
is the true America, and I'm wondering
who's the bigger ass, him spouting
or me listening, when my stare
falls on his two brats running
in and out of the screen door,
two boys who will likely
grow up to extend the reach
of their dad's simple mind.
But then I wonder what
would happen if his side won.
How bad could it be not to be
on the side of the bigger truths,
not even on the side of facts, which
would seem some kind of default
but is not, apparently? It would be
to believe the truth is tied as a child
is tied to its mother while the stars
spin crazily in their silent voids,
invulnerable, waiting to die, as we
are, but unlike us, unencumbered
with the memory of their rise
and fall. Now he's railing against
the gay agenda and refuses to use
any term but "sodomite," which gives him,
he thinks, a kind of patristic armor.
But after all, he is family,
and I let him go on, without further
correction, as the kids breach the door

once more, and I can see
how they could kill me, a grownup
who bandies language. Theirs
are the small eyes that peered
from the dark of caves that belonged,
as they feared, to merciless animals
we know now only from renderings,
and then only sideways, never head-on,
as if the observers devoutly wished,
after recording them, they would pass.

Elsewhere

I'm listening to the same birdsong over
and over. It's what the bird is putting
out there from inside the scalloped leaf
layers, then borne on the hot air
of a quiet afternoon. Something picks it up,
in some other tree, not the same song, but
consistent with its hammering repetition, only
elsewhere. That's the thing, isn't it?
Elsewhere. When Blake explained that Christ
was Imagination, what else did he
have in mind, but that the Son of Man
was elsewhere, working on a new gesture,
perhaps a sign as yet unknown to commentators,
which looked at first like legerdemain,
slipping through a hole only he could see,
to turn around in the air there, the highway
of birds, bearing witness, like any savior,
to its endless loops and curves.

The Attic

I'd thought the steps had shortened,
but the stair looked as if the indifferent sky
itself had offered a rippling rope ladder
like one of those dangling uncertainly over
the side of a tanker ship, so steep
was the ascent, so unlikely the salvation
from the sea. But that was a trick
of perception. True, the folding ladder
was shy a rung, its legs so far from straight
I imagined the odd, reversed knees of beasts,
before focusing on the rectangular hole,
like an inverted grave, upward into darkness.
Once there, I made my way over boxes,
the annals and souvenirs: pictures pocketed
in bill-flapped envelopes—dozens—yellow
on black like barriers at construction sites.
Then correspondence, some bundled and tied,
as if themselves in families, some loose, shiftless;
then envelopes alone, just a step above
empty wrappers; then more letters shed
of their envelopes, still making entreaties.
Past row on row of such a congeries, such remains,
I crawled like Nebuchadnezzar in that Blake
engraving, naked, self-absorbed, alone with rodents
that scratched and tumbled behind barriers,
along ledges and beams. It was there I found—
furnace ducts crisscrossing in secret order
like a train yard—the metal box that held
the means that took you. It called to me
like a heart carried over continents and centuries—

Shelley's or some totem encased by saints
in Boccaccio. But this terrible heart was forged.
I knew it was there, how it had followed me
year by year, from house to house.
I remembered just where among the junk.
On hands and knees, I approached, supplicant,
knowing how long it had waited, box worthy
of some hero, not me, but I couldn't help myself.
As if waiting for the moment to widen and
let me in, I reached out my hand in love.

Ode to Wilbur Mills

"He can't speak with you now, he's on the floor."

When the house next door went up
for sale, I wondered about the children
racing through the garden maze,
two little boys and a bony girl
skimming the boxwoods. Now another
yard sign appears across the street
before the lawyer's house with its blue gingerbread,
"New Price" affixed like a Post-It
(I didn't know there was an old one).
A workman's wooden ladder directs
the eye to messed, rotted shingles
and mottled underlayment
above the porch and a man there,
hands on hips, surveying the job ahead.
What if my poems find no place?
What if the house changes hands
and the ladder comes down
when all is fixed and rearranged,
when the oak behind the blue house
towers and becomes, for a moment, still?
I stare at sameness and seem to see
back through the layers, and the thought
comes to me of Wilbur Mills
giving a press conference from the dressing room
of his stripper darling,
the ruinous audacity that drew
a blessing—the silent applause of divinity.
I remember his bespectacled face
emerging from its mask after thirty years

to squint from the past into the camera,
and the idea likewise emerges that
it's like that, the peering beyond thinking
of the god of love, the terrible god
of faith and wreckage.

Treehouse

I look up and imagine living in the tree,
not as a squirrel starting, fidgeting
before a mortal leap, or as a crow
keen to fold its negative parasol,
still less an owl in whose stereopticon
no grace intrudes to rescue prey.
But I would climb up, as I did
with my brother, and build a treehouse
in the sweetgum limbs. The twisting
slats in our ladder led to the level
planks from which rose walls and ceiling.
There was even a window, put in
with much effort, to keep an eye
on trouble which, like innocence,
was always by and loved the shade
we cast, a reverse spotlight into which
it stepped like the host of an old variety
show to have us know it was starting.

After All

I once had a girl, sang the Beatles.
I had one who was high maintenance,
though she admired a local man
who ripped engines from new Jaguars
and replaced them with Chevy V-8s—
so unlike her own philosophy.
I loved her for the troubles, although
of course they became a liability by and by.
Even as my poem takes shape,
drying on the legal pad, I note
that some expressions ("although"
"of course," "by and by") exist only
to true the bias of neighboring words.
Before you know it, a tale is spun,
a form imposed, and feelings
imprisoned. Dostoyevsky
could not have come up
with a more disturbing heroine
than the one who emerged
from our falling in together.
It would be merely literary
to provide examples here of her
vitriol: many was the time I stiffened at it,
only to be melted by an artless word.
If it is possible to forgive
such a woman and in the process
to forgive myself why do I
hang back? I thought she was
peerless, the real deal. What was
I thinking, you may rightly ask?

When you stop to consider it,
everything is a test. In failure
you step forth just like the beloved
in the Shakespeare sonnet, except
that you aren't the beloved anymore.
You are just a person who has incurred
certain consequences that fold in
with natural changes and after a while
become indistinguishable from them.
If it is possible to forgive,
doesn't the pain return for another bow?
Doesn't the feeling of degradation likewise
follow the memory of drama?
I had learned from Mozart
that forgiveness is an attribute of deity:
Lazarus coming back from decomposition
at the summons of Christ;
Semele unblasted, her limbs refitted,
the gorgeous head reattached to its neck
before the presto of reanimation
and the trudge to Olympus. And yet,
isn't it said that the torn sing anyway,
the head as in a trance, slowly mouthing
the O of astonishment at having
returned to life, for what
could that life hold in this
new limbo? It was, after all,
just an idea of the more aggrieved.
After years, my girlfriend did get help
and yet, as Lowell remarked,
how terrible that such *Sturm und Drang*
resulted from a salt deficiency. I forgave
with what limited motive I could muster,

but she did not return to my life.
She was happy with the life she had
working on her golf swing
with her CEO husband. And I
was left to contemplate my partial act,
that bomb against nature
that didn't go off because only the trigger
ignited. But nature doesn't want
the return of the dead. Only we
do because the heart is an ironist,
which is to say, a nihilist,
because it will go to its grave believing
we were nibbled by happiness,
when sadness swallowed us whole.

Magic Marker

In my memory I hear the cries of poets
I knew or read years ago, fearing
the coming muteness of their verses,
their growing irrelevance in snow after snow,
storm after storm and even more, the long,
monotony of unassisted time, the triumph
of inertia over will. Japanese
maples filter the sunlight into infinite
gradations until, as noon passes over
into afternoon, that green shade
in the Marvell poem unites with
the green thought somewhere in imagination's
forest. It's here those cries rise
into a soughing that almost immediately
subsides. When she knew death was
soon to come, a former artist's muse
once told me that whenever she saw
a sign that proclaimed, *Jesus Saves,*
she would pull over and reach
for a Magic Marker she kept in the console
for just such occasions, and making
her way to the sign in question
would add the single word: *string.*

School of the Americas

I forgave my aunt for boasting she knew
Lt. Calley and for banishing her daughter
to a home for unwed mothers at nineteen.
(*Finishing school* was the phrase we heard.)
The girl, now nearing middle age, would be
somewhere in America. But where?
New facts show their traction now
that these relatives have died off
and left the home stretch unimpeded
by their last emergencies. What I couldn't
forgive was the time this aunt woke
my brother and gripping him by the forelock
hissed he was "stupid" to have kicked
my uncle, a full colonel, the day before,
as he made ready to leave for his job
with the infamous School of the Americas,
where he taught history to killers.
He met the blow with a look and made
no reply, but reinstated the military tone
with such enhanced indifference
we came to regret our vacation there.
That summer I pursued my cousin,
an in-the-know pre-teen who had already
trained brown doe eyes on boys.
My brother moped and never after
seemed as triggered by mischief.
My uncle took his pension by an Arnold
Palmer course near the base,
a retired general on the far side
of the water trap. I couldn't forgive

whatever it was that planted the cruelty
in her voice—or my uncle's silence.
But the butterfly effect, secret timing,
and indirection spread and toughened
death's vine. If to forgive is to
bring back to life, let them lie
in the peace of mistaken privilege,
if peace it is. As for me, I can't
and I don't. Let death be the lesson
again, as it was in the beginning,
so that what it is without them
unfolds in love's stead, under the sky
where I lie back, eyes open, taking
into my body breath that is all mine.

Song for Tom

For Tom House

Let's say Jesus made an offer:
the songs but without the voice—unless
you count a finishing sandpaper
voice drier than Dylan's, less able
to hold a note than Leonard Cohen's.
Would anybody give his whole life,
complete with anonymity, disease,
divorce, penury—to accept such a gift?
"Some nights I can't feel my feet," you said,
"when I'm performing." Here you swept
your freckled arm as if to say, "All this..."
revealing street shoes flat-footed
next to a barstool. "I'm afraid I'll topple
from the stage and crash on a drunk
divorcée at the first table." When *Esquire*
profiled you in the '90s I thought
at last for your sudden fame erupting
from the obscurity we shared.
Eventually, obscurity lapped the fame,
but the fame flexed into myth
and when I saw you last, now forty years on
in uncharitable Nashville, you
had just sold the rights to your catalog
in return for future deals, nominal,
niche, your record company a website.
You still trekked by bus to Calgary
or some South Carolina hamlet
just to let a college or a local jock
have at you for an evening. By the time

you had bought it all with flesh's coin
you were a coterie star. And when
the musicians sat around, you observed,
there was no way to stanch the booze.
Jarrell remarked how in driving out
our demons we should beware
of driving off our angels too.
It is the obligation of service,
you explained, to propitiate the angels.
So like the shards they sing of,
your songs reclaim the territory,
the torn maps, creased trailers,
the sadism of the banal against which
real yearnings cross, forging destinies
from lives as memorable as wallpaper
in songs as sturdy as Biblical wood.
Such your genius, to rasp our fiascos
far out into that other world
that, like the part in Jimmy Carter's hair,
reverses the whole head, and all that stands
behind that head—a fact detected
when a photographer from the press pool
compared the newest negatives
with all the stock on file.

Bald Man with Poodles

When the cemetery trees were pinched
over by the storm that day, their rootballs
rose and sat like strange, hairy globes
of dirt and rotted wood, and beside them,
the freshly excavated craters where once
they stood. The first to arrive were afraid
to look in, for fear some protruding bone
would confirm how wanton was air
in the service of death, and so snatch
the boutonniere from the lapel of the man
walking by, the bald man with a poodle
attached to each arm. Everyone knew
his mate abandoned him; no one knows
why. In spite of the trees he walks by.
It is the ordinary that sucker-punches.
Sunlight ricochets off his shiny head.
The dogs, like animals made from balloons
by an unfunny clown at a children's party,
would prefer the smell of turds and grass
to affection given on account of their beauty.

Heresies of Self-Love

I have known more narcissists
than is healthy for a man my age.
They've come in all sizes and shapes
but they've had one thing in common:
they lacked the ability to imagine
briefly that they were not themselves,
which in just about any shorthand
translates to a lack of imagination.
And yet, it was seldom unadulterated,
that love; rather it was a desire to self-
dance, as Shahid used to do in clubs,
a student assistant designated
to chauffeur and then to follow him
onto the dance floor with—I kid you
not—a full-length mirror so that
he could enjoy himself to the max.
Or take my friend, the visiting writer
in but one of a thousand skirmishes,
scoring points off a prissy senior
professor who rose to take issue
with her at dinner. "George," she
said, slicing the table with the blade
of a look, "you say *one-grotesque-thing-
after-another.*" As a poet friend said,
when I told him this story—how she had
dissed modesty with a flick: "She is
a very stupid woman." They were performers,
and we felt delighted at what seemed
an unreachable freedom. But not all
were so entertaining as to be merely

benign. Blake, who is infallible in such
matters, said that Satan is the ego,
the imagination's surrender to bounds.
My college roommate bears this out:
an only child, he learned self-love so
hopeless and pure he wouldn't kiss girls
unless they brushed their teeth first,
for which purpose he brought along,
and handed over, a spare toothbrush,
then waited on the makeout couch
for their return, if they bothered.
If they didn't, no matter. When I
happened to mention an attractive
classmate who had given up art
to marry a much older Florida man,
he replied without a hint of irony:
"I copulated with her once."
Nor did other than natural fabric
touch his epidermis. Even boiled cotton
seemed an insult, as I learned once
on a boat ride at Kerr Lake when he
stripped off the lavalava covering
his vitals before my startled wife,
then posed, an escaped art-class model
buck-naked on the prow of the motorboat,
hands on hips, eyes on the horizon,
as tethered skiers skipped by.
I was sure we'd all regret our ill-
starred vacation when the Coast Guard
turned us over to the vice squad.
But even a temple falls into disrepair
when the last priest enacts the aging
of window and beam. Like my superior

colleagues, I used to frown at these
lurid cautionary tales, but nowadays
what I really regret is the way
the parallel lives erased my own.
I smiled at the bravado and the times
remembered because of an image or a story.
But when I speak to this past
and hope to hear my name returned
in the voice of another, what I get
instead is the sound of tires slicing wet
pavement, and maybe there's a wind
lifting the heavy racks of leaves
and letting them down again,
maybe a bird hunched and invisible
near the dry trunk, the shielding
bark, whose song is the bread-
and-butter of any strange, nighttime fowl.

The Slug

When they found him in bed,
facing up, the police were hesitant
to rule my brother's death a suicide.
The pistol lay there yes, in his left hand
and yes, there was an exit wound
so blood had equal opportunity to sop
the bed from either side and mix its
metallic odor with the smell of gunpowder.
But any habitué of *CSI* would know
the perp will remove the bullet, if possible,
and so the cops were suspicious,
unwilling to say what we feared most.
Instead, they bracketed their skepticism
and went about collecting other evidence,
taking samples and pictures, measuring
the ricochet crater in the dresser trim,
as his body lay, like *savasana* in yoga,
a difficult pose because you have to
commit to stillness against every itch
or urge to rearrange the limbs and bring
them into closer alignment with the inanimate.
They found the note, beer cans, rifled
files. I myself discovered the note too,
reversed, embossed on a blotter—and clear
only on the reverse side, so that you
had to hold the eerie dispatch to a mirror
and read it like Leonardo's journals,
those discourses disallowed to commoners.
But what could be more common
than the wish to spare more pain,

as halting words, especially, arrive
one at a time, to serve? It was not
until hours after the fact that
the coroner ordered the body moved.
Then they found it, the bullet. In its
journey out the .38 barrel and through
my brother's wits, it had bounced
like a pinball around the machine
of the bedroom, furniture its bumpers,
and come to rest. Falling back on it,
he had both hit a bullseye and written
a mystery before the lead was cool.
The cops were amazed at the dead man's
surprise and crowded around the slug
like miners around the Hope Diamond,
for whom, as with the real miners, there
was no profit to be had from finding
such a conspicuous, untradeable treasure.

The Courage of Unspeakable Acts

My father spoke of it, hunched
there on the balcony. I offered him
a cigarette, but he waved me away.
He had officially kicked the habit
but he wasn't so good at hiding
his stash—at least not to me.
I had smoked a dead man's pack
that I found in a jacket: I knew
the day would come, and it did.
Not far away, a Confederate cemetery
got up in emblems and flags was but one
lost cause. The sons of my mother
were another, and one day my wife
turned to me at dinner and declared
my habits were a "slow suicide."
The phrase reminded me of the caption
in Bishop's poem about her timid aunt.
She remembered the phrase describing
a man slung on a cannibal spit: "long pig"—
what at *National Geographic* passed as wit.
The crack in the sidewalk soon finds earth.
There were sidewalks below us, but no
people. The smoke from my Lark merged
with the larger breeze. It was evening.
I didn't know what light my father
was looking at when he said,
"I can't get over the courage it took.
No one ever talks about it."
At that moment we were called

back inside, and I flicked the cigarette
into the night, kept the smoke in my lungs
as long as possible, like life itself,
then held the door for my father.

The Translator

He didn't have his own poetry
but he had that of others
which he translated. And those
versions became his *oeuvre*,
the work of his life, although
it was also the work of others.
In this way, he kept himself to himself,
and that public-private divide
others find both necessary and a great
human enigma (think Chekhov, Woolf),
he dismissed altogether.
His translations became famous for
their clarity and prudent word choice.
He won praise for not imposing himself
on his authors, but for disappearing
into the service of the art. What
nobody saw was what a great poet
he had become. His private life
was always the theme, and every
work was a masterful elegy for what—
now singing in an alien tongue—
it was no longer. In the end, he did
all that a man can do who wishes,
as Emerson said of every man,
to justify himself, who would otherwise
stumble on the way to success
and fade, unexpressed and obscure.

Yes Way

The studio was coming along. She'd had
racks installed to store the paintings,
an a.c. brought in to supplement the meager
cool that never seemed enough, when the sun
bore down and heated the blinds to scorching.
She'd rearranged the track lighting,
set up a stereo so she could listen
to chamber music there, in that chamber.
And an unbreakable lock: not to forget that.
On the other hand, there was the time
away, putting out feelers in the big city.
There were the close friends and death:
one gone and one waiting. No way
was there work to be done in the interstices
of these events. Then the hoary father
whose self-love was so indomitable
he threatened to outlast the room, as if
he might become, finally, the first immortal.
Why feel mugged by his demise?
She started to work again, to bury
him over and over, to catch
multiple caskets escaping in a black sky,
or was it to wave them on?
In any case, the sky cleared and there
was nothing in the way at last but
the self imprisoned in its freedom.
Perhaps the moribund would last a little longer
yet. Perhaps the cancer would lose the code.
Then what? The President goes nowhere
without the man carrying the football.

But that is no guarantee that
anyone will survive a first strike.
The paintings piled up. Someone would
have to investigate new storage.
But where? Who could build a rack
strong enough to bear such events
as the canvases imagined, then hid
to keep out the uninitiated, those
critics and pundits whom everyone sees
at openings, who put the drunken artists off
with their pickled scowls and solemnity?
But it was the way to go, filling the racks
until they groaned instead of the psyche.
Though unseen, it was destined to be
the best show in many a season. The work
would go on, as it always did, from there.
The President turned to wave as he
boarded a plane and everyone was dazzled.
Only a photograph recorded the other man,
unsmiling, standing with his briefcase.

Dalman Flowers

I wrote the same poem twenty times
and tossed it out each time, unable
to figure out what I wanted to say.
It was in equal measure overwhelming
and vague, like a lot of things
having to do with origins, and both
the immensity and insignificance of people
for whom years proved a thicker blanket
than the ground ever was. I looked
at my model poets for guidance. Cavafy
suggested I use only small anecdotes
with sharp details—the rest would be
suggested through understatement.
Leopardi showed you have to notch it up
into the general air where individual
men and women lose their serial numbers
and join the human stream, at which
point your poem is a slow wail
of acquiescence. My poem began
with a man on an unpainted porch.
He was wearing overalls and looking
at the dry fields across the road. His son
would die of complications from polio.
His wife would succumb to a stroke
and die wedged between the refrigerator
and the kitchenette counter in a trailer.
He himself was awaiting earth departure
with Lou Gehrig's Disease. I remember
how he used the heel of one hand
to push the thumb of the other

in order to get the Pontiac door to open
in the hospital parking lot. I don't know
what put me in that scene, but to this day
the shock of that image still registers,
as does his floral name: Dalman Flowers.
And so I turn again to Leopardi, where I find
sunflowers of the Marche buttering the fields,
as he set forth to find the troubles that fed
his real Muse, and the loss of identity
that gave him, in its place, a pure voice,
that made his sweet Silvia possible
and Romanticism itself—these things
waiting to meet him, later, in Rome.

from

The Red Tower

(2010)

A Life Preserver

He watches the light move in and out
behind the evening clouds and listens
to the wild duck's long, sad cadence,
interrupted by crows. He senses
the still air is indifferent
to these rituals. For all that,
he knows the connections there
are the nodes of moments
already deep in the braid
of a rope, coiled and put
in a public place under lock and key,
a life preserver, in case of emergency.

Harp

A bad painting, at once aggressive and shy,
connects its glassy, Alpine blue
with a utilitarian sofa beneath—where no one sits—
and that in turn to footstools
like toadstools leading away, becoming flagstones
that would take the eye the distance
across the domestic space of the room.
Leaves wobble by the window opening
and across from that window
on the fifth story balcony above the sidewalk
(where immigrants drift in shoots and eddies)
a young, bespectacled mother puts out the wash:
blouses and leggings on metal dowels,
underwear in an aluminum rack tub.
She disappears and returns with an armload
of baby wash, though where this will go,
now that the racks are full, is not clear.
But distribute them she will,
paying no mind to the encroaching garden
from the balcony above, nor the slag
of toys piled on the balcony below.
Nor of me, sitting by a wooden harp, in a room
not mine, thinking of hot, loser towns
where I am no longer, of years imagined
when I never was. One child's dress, an ever-
serviceable blue cotton smock, says it all,
hanging four-square from the balcony rail,
as if in the absence of its little owner, billowing,
it took that absence on a journey.
Pointless speculation, says a contrapuntal voice,
and yet that is what I did with my life.

Roofers

At the knock and sound of my name
I would rise and sit before my father's meal—
fried eggs, grits, link sausage, canned
biscuits—watching him pore over,
then fold, the *Morning Herald* by his place.
In the still dark we would cross town
in an old Chevy, pick up a man
by name of Whitey or Buck,
and we would sit, three to the bench,
through lightless streets to an old house
below Forest Hills, or some mill-hand's place,
hard against Duke Forest.
Pretty soon, we were roofing, gouging off
the outdated, loose, and rotted shingles,
flinging them over the dark edge,
laying down new ones in tight array,
nail-lined, error-free. We woke
the neighborhoods those Saturdays.
Hammers in holster, we stood in the midst
of rooftops as the colors came on,
first the long-ago rose, then a strange green
as my father, turning, bent to his row
and one by one, from between
his silent lips, pulled the nails.

Rorty

Raised by Trotskyites, he had a soft spot
for the writerly reactionaries: Eliot,
Larkin, poets steeped in Original Sin,
for whom poetry was the *scala sanctorum*
and the best lines ineffable.
Not for him, the abolisher of Truth,
the materialism of words. He loved
not only what they could do, but what they
aspired to do. One day, setting
down his bourbon after a seminar meant
to engage unkempt, querulous supernerds,
he told me that Allen Tate had been his
favorite teacher at the U. of Chicago.
Grinning, he told how each class
consisted of Tate reciting a single poem,
in his sonorous, waterlogged baritone,
then pausing, adding, "Isn't that beautiful?"

The Apartment

Through the window I saw, in a canted plane,
an apartment building rise—stonework, ironwork
and detailing where every other window
extends into a balcony. The penultimate
floor bore a laced cincture, and I was reminded
of my vertigo stepping out from the top
of Trajan's Tower in Rome years ago.
The guardrail stopped at knee-level,
and the tower floor itself did not exceed
three-feet wide. At your back, granite;
out beyond the eyes: air's abyss. Now,
a convenience store occupied street level,
but the air was a void all the same.
A sculptor, on commission, carved the spiral
of the Emperor's conquests among the Etruscans,
the Dacians, and the Goths—like all killing
utterly repetitious in the ringing iron,
the screams of horses, the helmeted bodies.
At some point, the eyes following the spiral
could no longer take in the scope of victory,
but the vanishing point was no less bloody
than the start, the swords no less blunt.
By contrast, the top floor I saw—tilted
and tiled—had only a rail and no place
out from the window to stand upon. Already
windows on either side were indistinguishable
from skylights. Who stood at that rail
saw boulevards stretching all the way
to the inhospitable suburbs. Just so,
saints were said to emerge from their cells
and pause, before going forth out of the spirit,
in their rope belts, into the stony forests.

The Ferry

There doesn't seem much point in following
the ridge that trails off until the cloud
absorbs the rock. I had been trying
to make an image for that change,
how the hawk merges with the bare madrona,
how the slap of the motorboat hull
is followed by the long, rolling wake.
After lunging repeatedly, each in choke-chain,
porch dogs thought the better of it
and rounded their day with a sleep.
A crow came toward me on a road
as if I were no longer wild.
The ferry plowed on without a variation
and felt almost formal in its transit,
almost a man finally in compliance
with orders sent down long ago.

The Red Tower

For two years I drove by a mountain
and wondered how long it would take
to tunnel through using a teaspoon.
That's how dead my brother was.
No, more. And I thought the young
Yeats was wrong when he wrote
that God talked to those long dead.
I imagined a blinking tower
on a mountain: the red light pulsed
but raised no one. Because even if
God talked to the dead, what could
He possibly say to them?
What could He possibly say?

Theology

Downstairs I hear Jill on the phone
with the oncologist. They could be
discussing theology or how to keep the strike
going without breaking the company.
After all, whole neighborhoods,
like unsecured cargo, know the rough slide
from rail to rail. She laughs

and I take it the doctor, a cautious young man,
stands momentarily in the ray
that shoots down from an opening
in the cloud cover.
Perhaps they shared a joke about age,
that party boat steaming westward
where the sun, always setting,
pokes through here and there looking,
as it were, for daylight.

Wild ducks below skim off across the sound.
Their cries answer the question
I would have put to the man,
but I see where they're going with this
and the thing, animal to animal,
they carry into the weather.

Thinking about Logan

for Michael Waters

I marveled at Logan's late poem
celebrating the bride of his youth,
the fiery anticipation and shyness
with which they stared at each other's rings,
before crossing the river, hills rising before them.
The future, which has the advantage
over a poet's love, manages to beckon
with the silvery twist of a treetop
as fall arrives, in garish and particular ways:
sunlight glaring off the dust of windshields
without, the oily grime of breath within,
dust in the tobacco leaves drooping
where the reaper comes, an Hispanic worker
perched on the driver's seat, itself leaning out
over the soil like Demosthenes' lantern.
When asked who I wanted to see when I first
visited Frisco, I replied without hesitation,
"Logan." My teacher said, "Oh, no, you don't.
He's foraging garbage cans in the Castro,
these days, a bum." Outed and teetering, he
stood there at the finale of a festival not
many years before. Yet not many before that
found a new image for Jesus's cross-mate
nailed to time on Cabrini Green. I had
my own first wife to dazzle with the new man
I was, and I knew the human thrill
of those first rings, before the animal snapped
and the brain slid to the back of the skull;
before the heart on derelict pilgrimage

could put two garbage can morsels together.
I didn't see him then, and not long after,
he was gone. What followed coarse fact was
the gradual blurring of detail, followed in its turn
by forgetting altogether (my students, for instance
draw a blank). But I remember the shiver
he wrote about, that passion holding desire
between the zig of attraction and the zag of doubt,
the young husband offering his face to that
of the girl, who looked up from the ring, not
finding anywhere the stranger they were to meet.

from

The Pilot House

(2009)

After Reading

I put down the book thinking
how purity is a curse, how it
puts us off the human
for whom it better fits
to turn away from the shore
in favor of the garbage and the grief.
I remember standing in the nave of St. Peter's
looking at the smooth, dead body of Christ
held in Mary's arms and secretly admiring
the madman whose hammer
chipped the same marble that made
Michelangelo such a monster.

Patience

He knew the chorus and later,
learned the other dances.
Large ships no longer outside his life
looked set free, their reflections
as majestic as their bodies. He knew
that lapping and the beach smell,
the water coming ashore as seabirds
waited, spending their brief lives
in patient attending. *Pazienza*, said the sign
as he entered the library, handing
the librarian a slip of paper
for a poet so long dead that stars
were different when he looked up,
that his language died
waiting for the new stars.

Lincoln

Near the tip of Lincoln's nose,
Cary Grant had one second of the sensation
that draws swallows to a height
where they no longer make the effort
to propel themselves but glide
like their distant cousins, the buzzards
stirring the sky between cloud and corpse.
As perspectives go, it's hard to argue
with circle and sweep, and at intervals
they let go a stately peep, the way a nickel
dropped from the Empire State Building
hits the pavement harmlessly between
taxis: one in use, the other going uptown
beyond the river, into the private streets.

The Gulf

Back in the day you could lie in bed
until the sun had punched through
the low, graphite cloud cover and been
well on the way to its own personal best
and still get a day's work done. Tragedy
went with indolence, loss was all-providing.
You could stand in front of the Easter
Island slab of an ATM and get meaning.
You could toast the air, never worrying
whether a beloved could occupy the same space.
That was the morning, when the river
decided to give itself up to the gulf.
When the riverboat hand, eyeing
the swells, called up to the wheelhouse,
saying, "Cap, are you seeing this?"

The Pilot House

I hear a hammer down the road
sounding the wood, and inside, my daughter
at her computer making sounds half-music,
half self-amusement. The paper
on my breakfast table describes rockets
flying in and out of Israel, in and out of Lebanon.
It reminded me of that time I went home
with Teresa Greenberg, whose dad
owned the only Rolls in town.
The Six Day War had started. Her father,
a squat and burnished contractor,
rose to grunt at me and immediately
resumed his place before the console TV.
There Moshe Dayan's pirate's patch
made the good eye the focus
of our world, a world put sorely away,
an old uniform with its service medals
waiting for the grandson who could
hold the whole thing up like a chart,
telling you what each ribbon and medal
signified. Years after what might have
happened followed what did, an oil tanker
steams by, the tall pilot house seeming
to inspect the trees, then sending smoke
into the low clouds, before sailing on
to the mountains beyond the treetops.

Wised Up

It's as if some middle were erased,
the mountaintops with their peaky drifts
down which slide wrinkles of ice
but no flanks and no base: just air
pretending to be sky as if participating
in that color, that all-leveling blue.
When my philosophy professor found
himself on a panel with the Dalai Lama
what he really wanted to do, he said
was to ask him to levitate
so that he could sweep his hand under
like a kid who has wised up,
debunking the magic, finding the wires.

Moulin

As I near the screen door I hear
Glenn Gould fighting his way
out of the basement, with Bach
as his staccato commander.
I can't tell if this is for my attention
or God's, or the Gestapo's, but I find
myself thinking of the French
resistance hero Jean Moulin
having heard my father-in-law say,
over a candle-lit table, among guests,
how haunted he was by Moulin's refusal
to talk, even under torture. What secret,
he wondered, had no exchange value?
That made even zero, by comparison,
a safe stuffed with papers?
It was the kind of secret Bach suggested
to crazy Glenn Gould, when like a sheepdog
he dashed from side to side
on the keyboard, compressing the oxygen
of the music, until I made a clearing
for his dead master's silence
that rose up after him and squeezed
through the threshold, just as I was crossing,
going the other way.

The Contest

I get detailed emails from my friends
describing events long ago. They copy
each other as the past is brought out
for another bow. They copy me,
though it's clear I haven't the memory
for the sequences, personnel, or the shading
of events, and so my contributions
are of necessity general and brief.
For all that, my memory's as stocked
as a survivalist's freezer in a '70s suburb.
I remember the tenor of particular
howls piecing the helpless air outside
beyond our open summer windows.
I recall a war once fought over a beer
that was really a spat about power,
as sex is, placed in front of justice.
And of course there was that time
my brother passed out at five,
the piss that ran spiraling down the chair leg
to form a puddle on the linoleum.
It was the first seizure, soon managed,
but I remember our frantic faces
as we crossed back and forth, small and dark
across his dilated pupils, the eyes
seeming not to move at all, like a contest
under way to see who was toughest,
who had the most to lose by blinking.

Immortal Soul

When the cancer rose to his brain,
my father started talking in terms
of his "immortal soul," which was unlike
the old talk of that gentle man.
One day, near the end, though wasted
to a bag twist, he went berserk
and lunged from his hospital bed
driving the nurses from the room,
as he wheeled his bed like a wagon
between himself and his tormentors.
In split-tailed hospital gown
he whirled and caught me coming
through the door. He had just
got his hand around the TV stand
and was about to pull the set,
complete with its soap opera, onto the floor,
when I stopped him. Then the look
of betrayal—so uncharacteristic—
settled in his face and hardened
the cool blue eyes. Taking hold of my arms
until we were locked in a struggle
like crabs dancing on the grave
of free will, he cried, "Don't you fear
for your immortal soul? Aren't you afraid?"
Finally exhausted by the manic urgency
he collapsed back into the same bed,
his wagon, taking him to the end.
Which was three days later. Rounded up
too late from a pointless meeting, I arrived
in time only to barge past the door

of the neighbor resident, an old woman
of whom I had been mostly unaware
and heard someone, a relative,
who held a picture between them, say,
"See? It looks just like you."

from

Two Estates

(2009)

At Todi

Clouds merge with stone.
Pigeons grip moss that trims the stone.
As hard as their roots, trees
rise like statues, and the grass
they dapple in the short run
the hills pick up as an effect, and spread.
At a curve's far reach, you meet
a shrine placed by shrewd peasants
to defeat expectation:
energies are already transforming
hard trees into their harmless shadows.

Never Forget

A standard dove would gargle
all day, gnats dangle their pulsing clusters
like water-balloons. And the ground
be overrun with ants and scarabs
rearranging the earth. Figs
about to touch ground from the most extended
branch would note
how the necropolis corrects dissolution
with architecture. How domes
rewrite hills, and fields, grown and cut,
reduce the river's pull
where gravity is quietest and most
conspiratorial, a drift
content that a single painter restore it
from allegory to realism. Clouds
would process their variations
across the countryside all day.
What both bird and butterfly did would go
by the same name. And that ecstasy
pouring from the stone would pass
through wheat's variations,
when the mower appeared mounting the hill,
its red dome and puff of smoke
so like the scythes of the painters.

Into the Wall

An anvil-shaped cloud
spreads its iron shadow
across the hill adjacent to our town.
As on a floor viewed upside down,
other clouds, in turn, suggest
figures of the moment,
requiring only the arrival
of the next bit of future to cancel
the suggestion. The struggle
is ancient: clouds' agon drives the painter
into the wall, attempting impossible
compressions proper to time beyond
a lifetime. Here, where the sound
of a scooter merges with a wasp's nest,
a pack of flies beats up a swallow—
until the next frame. Or the classical
head turns with its look
of a god disappearing into time:
things are as they are,
turning in middle air,
and as they will be,
emerging from the rock.

Campanile

The stones they shouldered above
stay above: their quarters are still
the plain, impersonally stuccoed flats
snail-clustered across the valley.
They know *up* always ended where
a campanile diffused sound and figure
meant to charm God, or else
to arrest Him. The faces are familiar:
Mussolini had one—and Gramsci—
below-wall faces atop solid, compact builds.
Today the sky is repeating something about
its clouds, how they were one stimulus
for the adulation of the flesh,
for Fra Angelico's heaven-limiting
bodies. Any heaven from this moment
takes on the likeness of bodies
who passed from the labors demanded
of stones, and rose again, matching hills
in whose folds and valleys swallows
making their barrel-and-rollout
menace the tassled wheat.

Vespers

Wind carries off the slighter
birds, after which a purling of doves
adjusts the evening. An owl stands
quiet as a pine cone when a blade of light
breaches the hilltop and is gone. Behind me,
a compact car carries compact profiles
to town. Only a cloud, like a lipstick kiss
left on a mirror, offers
its supplemental farewell to the unbroken haze.
This is the final atmosphere
of a work day: not great bindings
but the modest affinities: bread
crossing the table,
as the jet engine overcomes the dove.

Combine Stopped in a Field

The tracks regulate sight where
the least genius for memory takes hold
the way Cornell dolls fill a square.
Pigeons erupt from their blocks
to see what their arcs hold when,
at the end of theatrics, they return
to their destiny: a square on the other
side of the same minute. Looping
explanations fail to articulate
the general disorder we knew
as children, before steeps themselves
had an end. A hawk locates a thermal.
Only this-as-that favors this.
The same pigeon, as plump as a castle
could produce, springs once more,
its body in the process constructing
two sides to encase the eye's moment.
Midsummer. To exonerate memory
for the erasures of past moments
was the easy part. Faces were
like frescoes seeming to derive
their appeal from disappearing,
even as they continued to illustrate
the higher orders and structures, as if
either could exist minus walled flesh.
Yet the field's stupor all by itself
outstrips the mower's desire to stand
down from the turning of that
world to its successor. The equator
of his waistline moves majestically

in space. The hawk is gone, or else,
a fine coincidence of form shuts sight out
altogether. The combine will start back,
managing the pain, supplying the field
details that flow from its choosing.
But that is another part of the summer,
still becoming, still planning to impress
the mind with its sequential shades:
the sudden incandescence of fields,
followed by their relapse to green,
the inevitable snaggle of vines that
would suture a bursting mountain shut.

Gate by a Boat Pond

Like a logo, one tree shading the gate
previews a whole silver arboretum
along the southern shore. These make up
a larger, more approximate bank to secure
the meadow against water's encroachments,
though the opposite is more likely:
that earth will seal the place of reflection,
ruining all the spin-offs of heaven
that can be assembled from sparse sky
whose only cloud's a thumb-smudge
of white. Why not then, a formal gate,
a square, old-fashioned lock hungry
for graphite, that will nonetheless
show the bars of heaven falling away
at your shoulder's heave-to
and the three fettered boats scarcely moving
in their cove, their oars blistered,
oarlocks empty as music lyres sticking
from the bells of discarded instruments?

Houses in a Necropolis

Pretty huts, cells of memory:
these dead were not put by
but elevated. The cloud's shadow
must first climb the walls,
then inch up and over wavy roofs,
unlike the scything sweeps of light
on a grave. The stone believes
the future is repetition, desirable
in itself, a hill as matrixed
and parceled as any Cézanne,
where the seasons roll unimpeded.
The stone encasing the star-
tilted skeletons knows the ochre
and browns and the limiting cases—
yellows and purples, as well as trees
and bushes, Germanic, obeying orders,
whether in forests or trimming
a cathedral's ground to secure
in nature what a trinity of chairs
could not, dulled by dust, or bursting
into flames. The stone is also the vault
from which the past cracks
its coffers, and the dead claim
neither justice nor business has
the same length as life, even as they
reach to lock in the embrace.
The stone is also the vault.

Engraver's Stone

A hint only of drawn clouds
projected annexes to the hills.
A callower light offered sunflowers
to a stadium. Now they too seem
merely additional, the overripe diva
whose arrival renews, for a moment,
the tone of bemusement in a bad restaurant.
A tractor struggles with a barnload of hay
to negotiate the steep ground separating
the known from the imagined.
Its swiveling amber
cautions only distant memories,
distant wars that grew holy changing
abundance to scarcity. The plow
becomes a roadside decoration,
disabled as a statue guarding a bank.
The engraver's tool was all forward momentum
until the hand was replaced,
and the stone stood as blank
as a ledge. Beyond this,
in humid day, clouds
begin to draw themselves,
as if there is a place for that
when there was no time
for the other.

Annunciation

From the belly, impossibly, horizons
and horizontals begin their reign.
Only the messenger is bracketed
from this by a parapet's opening.
But his head's melting vertical
is itself the message announced
in a constellation of trees.
The angel sees the girl is the equal
of it. His head intends a further
seriousness as if, in lowering itself,
it had ceded responsibility
for vision. The messenger's wings,
half spread, show necessity
engaged in display, as easily
as ducks commence mating. Raised
in admonition, her hand aims
its invisible ray at the other's hand
raised in the classical pose,
for the classical passes now
as human only, and she would guard
this humanity, even as she accepts
the other assignment: to return god
to flesh so longed for, and the life
that burns, striving and ending.

Not the Tall Grass

Even spotted with sarcomas, leaf-mold,
egg-cases, and the clean-bore holes
left by worms, the fig tree
sees to its own dead indiscriminately
with a seam's load of fruit.
Mounting sun-warmed church stones
miles away one could rise to its window-
apertures to locate spirit's participation
where green bounded green, and a hill
became plural. For on one side
bars of rain advanced on the promontories,
announced by sticks of lightning;
on the other, a field of sunflowers
like lungs before diving, stood
at fullest bloom for miles. We
came to affirm an identity in stone—
doves' headquarters, our
decoration—until earth could yield a second
figure equal to our mass, as granite
and marble trimmed the spirit with irony,
and the eyes could be startled again
there, where the mower stopped.

The Landscapist

But which are the joints that unseam
valleys when you cut them?
Gradations of tillage,
trees dotted in amazement, patterns,
accountings, conceptions laid out
with gentlest effect? Though ground
is often chaos itself, in these motions
you dance in an imagined time
when time gone comes back,
irrepressible, joining field and sky
in an artless desire for restoration
after such bending. No other way
than to follow dependencies that tie
slopes to snake and snail,
rhythmic weeds competing with stone
towers for the scorpion's ennui.
Does death crook the arm in that
learned fashion? Then death is a genre
whose work renders all approximations
repeatable: a discourse of wheat.
Then you have offered your symbol
in a field ripening from boundaries
you make and stand within.

Qua

Foreground: wheat close up
and the morning's birds. Doves
packed in stone chatter brilliantly.
Background: gauzy, not much help:
hills are nets, each node a village.
By the cinquecento, the mariner myth,
like the bookish shepherd who lugs
a sacked lamb across the landscapes
of countless murals, had set in: time-
as-sea, as much time as a net lets pass,
until waves rise up into question marks
before rolling on to find, everywhere,
stony coast materializing from mist.
And sea-as-*si*, that term of assent, that
agreement—so long in coming—to let
stones take the place of waves.

Mowing Day

Just when grass dreams it isn't wheat,
over a rise, like Hannibal's elephants,
combines begin gouging road-width
channels through a meadow.

Midsummer, mid-morning.
Fallen clouds still hug the river,
reluctant to join the cirrus stream
challenging a distant vapor trail

(though both directions stand
to benefit from the contrast).
Gone to seed, the wheat's a brass
plaque offered to one hillside

by another, itself eclipsed by an acre
of no-longer-Impressionist sunflowers.
Machines whose grunting fools
only sparrows, sweep all before them,

iron tusks bobbing, leaving only
a shimmering insect circumflex
floating over the cropped layers
and swifts glutted on the radiance

surrounding stone. But all's rising
until clouds become a vertical field
where ground and sky take out their maps
and get down to gesturing and pointing.

Piero's Resurrection

Of the four, two of the soldiers
face the viewer. Theirs are faces
belonging to citizens of the world.
The sensual body of one invites comparison
with Christ's body, which is inferior
and scarcely regarded—even as
it rises, even by him. His being
is situated in the face, itself tired enough
to be abridged to eyes. The pull
of the world is so strong that
resurrection of the body
no longer counts as salvation.
The women, for example, who slept
with the soldier knew caresses were nothing
without the indolence of perishable love.
The other soldier, whose amiable goatee
hints at a sophistication and *savoir faire*
beyond his station, holds in both hands
his useless pike, whose point seems to
lance the side of the nearest tree.
On one arm hangs a drooping shield,
. "SP" visible to the spectator, as if
even in Piero's time, one had only to add
et cetera to explain the derivation of force,
by degrees, from vegetable nature.
The other figures exist to supplement
sleep with blindness: while the left one
cradles his face in his hands to show
how weariness occludes awareness,
the other actually faces the god

but of course can see nothing except
the inside of his eyelids. One must say God
is not as fine as these figures who have,
by casual descent, let consciousness go
in return for their ordinary beauty.
At this, the eye wishes to true itself
like a carpenter's level, and rises to
the horizon extended from Christ's shoulders.
Two rows of trees close in, framing
him in an emblematic trapezoid.
To the row of young trees, Piero has
juxtaposed a mature row, suggesting,
because both lines slant centerwards,
that when the sequence of growth leaves off,
trees are free to become instruments
and signs with their own succession:
cross-to-crucifix providing the model.
Here at the painting's crux, thought
rises from the grave of thought,
asking: who else can wake
and move off from this sleep
from which gravity the cool,
weary Christ rises brandishing
the crudest of symbols—a stick
and rag that pull him clear of the dead?

Lemon Trees near Izzalini

One field holds back another:
one aggressive, torched with blossoms;
the other, shorn, vulnerable, seemingly
without alternative. It's the seemingly
weaker that defends its right to simplicity,
for the blossoms must also divulge their shame
before the continuing sun, in the pressure
of whose falling light they would be justified.
The simple proposes hungers simply met
in an economy of medium tones.
The lemon trees along the suture
draw a line such as the grocer
used to make on the bag
where he added sums, and his flourish
(his only flourish) summed up the shock:
that this was what distinction was
in a world of resistance and change.

Luna Park

A necklace of bulbs
invites the ordinary.
A crowd scene, not yet painted,
includes many shades of dark
against tablecloths under sail:
some pairs rise to enact the antique
dances of common memory. More
watch, mud-soled, rough, their stillness
policed by children. Still others dance
as if the past were no partner, nor a thing
with points situated along a thread
of duration, but spinning off. As if the music
rode straight up on a column of air,
then fell back in fireworks, in intense
delight of its measure. The collective swallows
the individual, and the individual
unties the collective. Dogs prowling
margins invent a subculture and send
infiltrators among leg-mazes.
The summer constellations move
unnoticed behind strings of bulbs.
Love or some like tenacity
seeks no higher line of sight
than the usual face.
What are they to these same stars?
The stars are nothing to them.

Necropolis near Fiore

The land they need is undisturbed.
The labor in the fields shrinks them.
Clouds given off like ground exhalations
are no ornament to them, close-built.
Only two trees are needed to make
ironic shade. For us, no choice
but to stiffen for the wave swelling
in the back of minds racing forward.
They race too, reversed, from our charity.
The stone wall records its own decorum
for we would not approach unannounced,
nor speak names proper to be forgotten,
if only that the houses turn inward,
and no windows mend the individual dark.

Of a Party

I watched the sheet of fog
that had settled
on the slopes and cliffs hiding
lower earth from view
so that
spires and whatever else in part
denied the earth
let morning display their wish.

And I went to town at the start
of that burning
that revealed even trivial and loathsome
things, the night's dead
thrown up by the road:
a lizard pulling a moth's slack sails
into its craw, sagging green lawn bags
facing the stone necropolis.

The wonder of it was the mesh
of oblique things:
entities and force, process and bodies,
surface and wind, when the heat came on
as if a truth had been made plain
and someone the wiser
let that truth float, though it obscured,
at the moment of release, his own face.

Secret Hours

Like an equestrian act, a cloud
swivels, turns inside out, then rights
itself crossing Roman air space.
In the picture, Montale sits at a window,
smoking. Terrace candles,
in sympathy, blow smoke into
the air above the street. People gather
at an expat party of a sometime friend.
Will a Borghese come? An Agnelli?
Dr. Johnson said people were right
in public to prefer a duke to a genius
(though in secret hours they were
also right to steal off to please themselves).
Over the terrace, down in the street,
scooters streak by the methadone clinic.
In the next room, a fantastically tall
woman lifts a melon cube to her lips.
Her head is ringed with acanthus leaves.
A writer is forced to deliver the story
of his life in dreamy self-parody.
Like a bid at cards, his "I was there,"
washes away, as wine does,
what the past itself has failed to do.
Smoke blows over the lip of the terrace.
Montale is looking out the window,
where a lizard's push-ups
lose count of acts and silences.

Realm of Day

La Capella San Brizio

Some were escaping the grave,
some were standing around engaged
in the chit-chat of the totally nude,
buttocks of balled muscle, legs
as taut as grasshopper's springs
but only bent into an ordinary
pose above ground. Even those still
skeletons for whom the trumpeting
angels were most exacting labor,
smiled beyond the skull's grimace.

Everything else was less surpassing—
the glory of Christ a jet held out
to torch similar, but derivative halos.
Here and there Signorelli turned up
moments of indifferent cruelty: the impact
of truncheons on the weak, for instance.
Even his signature self-portrait reveals
not only Fra Angelico, his friend *al fresco,*
but the struggle of a man mugged and choked
at the unconcerned artists' feet.

Then a pack of German tourists
separated us, as their guide moved
to expound the False Messiah. Their faces
managed an unnerving sameness turning to
the Last Judgment, where devils, like secret
police, joined crowds milling about a piazza
to abduct both tradesmen and their wives.

The rapt spectacles and camera lenses
sheeted to a single, tilted pane such as
the sun makes in evening windows.

At which point I drew my hand
to my face and discovered there
a morning's smell unwashed enough
to enter a *duomo*, like the ardor
of those bodies, for whom spirit and flesh
were never wholly distinguished,
except to instruct the sight-impaired,
for whom dark was history's likeness,
and God's painted head: a flashlight
jabbing the smoke and the rubble.

Falling Giottos

Church bells send no picture but hover
in consciousness the way bees
slog away at the last sprigs
of wisteria. Spring-like October
warmth is equally for form's sake,
its month-long drought, a yawn.
But inside, the letting-go continues.
How quickly and with what fine
a sense, you hesitate to speak
as presently of still-present things.
It is a feeling unmarked in the woods
where a renunciation, also, continues
unabated, all the way to the solid
canopy of leaf and wood.
Sparrows too remote to be other
than mere silhouettes
follow each other down
paths degenerating into vectors
where every sighting becomes a *V*,
before which the mind enacts
the passion that figures possess,
when pictures share the destiny of a wall.

Uncrossed Passes

Just at that time of day
when the sky's most flamboyant cloud
stations its curls above
a pass made smooth and habitable
by a glacier's blade, the eye
considers the distant as heir
to the near and brings it forward
for the mind to lock in. It is
as if sight alone began a conversation
and the pass returned to snow,
or worse, to a route beyond,
where nonexistent saints draw
struggling carloads. But never
would you forget how the conversation
was only a pleasant, pointless roving
until a track emerged,
and that highway let forgetting be
the final act of love.

Poem at Midsummer

A breeze rustles the pines;
a commotion of doors.
But nothing stirs the air below
where a scarab beetle walks the plank
of a renovation and waits for the sun
to renew the dirt's nameless regimen.
You lie in a sugaring of sweat,
one nude leg proffering its gaunt bone
to what remains of dark
before infinite division returns
and splits the many from the one,
lighting the impatient towers.

Terra Cotta

The little bird outpaced the bigger bird
and it seemed for a minute
it would turn and attack.
But summer was well underway
and aerials reclaimed the airspace.
This life—half arboreal, half slab—
waits to give eyes what is denied
to bodies: a place to land that has
no memory of the pain of landing.
Terra cotta softens balconies' iron.
Stucco turns sunlight decorative,
a series of hues that funnel eyesight
to open doorways where shadows
take over the domestic space
in the name and shape of light.

Air Traffic

Even at mid-morning, a cock-crow
lacerates the valley air. Bees swarm
under the eaves, bypassing a watermelon
and sugar bowl well within reach.
As durable as one of Ulysses' men
the old artist heads for his shed,
chisel in hand. His granddaughter forgets
the scorpion sweep under the bed that set
her teeth chattering half the night.
Her days are as rich as a French count's,
an inventory of pranks and schemes
canceling the past's ridiculous void.
Today's air traffic, which is all duty,
seems all play, a general dalliance
that retreats to the open for cover.
Invisibility swallows a helicopter,
and modernity mutes the church bells
whose benediction too hangs in air
too short a time to become a soundtrack,
but long enough to cleave the day
into halves, with *then* falling flat
as a paving-stone, and *thereafter*
standing with its sheer face glistening.

Wind Picking Up

Hedge shade begins to reach across fields
unevenly: some stubble stays lighted
while other goes under. Trees no longer
take precedence over their shadows.
Though light is plentiful, gold
and some other associated hues withdraw
discreetly into stalk and ground.
The pond shimmers, reluctant to give up
its strip of sky. Hilltop houses begin
the transformation into silhouettes.
The wind, on the other hand, denies cover,
fretting the vineyards all night long.
Things turn to speech, and speech
to law, revising Moses and Hammurabi
on the knobby spines of badgers
and the ruffles of magpies. Darkness
is nothing to it, rumor is its angel
knocking at dreams, lifting the locks,
blowing oneness apart like a dandelion.

Discontinued Subjects

Sun just now spangling the slope's wet trees
shows no reason to wake the painter.
Nor the helmet brushes of hills emerging
through cracking banks of mist.
Let hawks' emptiness find the cure for gravity
on the back of this reddening light.
Let the insect millions, berserk
with necessity, cut through air
or clamber through soil. Enough
that they part the grass with thorax and hook,
presenting their hunger to the field of Mars.
All things resisting transformation:
hay-covered vipers, grasshoppers
in whose shade the leaf hefts its steel,
the brown lizard pulling sheets of stucco,
like skidding rugs, under its belly,
turn away from the sun and each other
with an indifference that acquires its own
passion and goes about in spite of itself
hallowing the surfaces and depths alike.

Ellipsis

Like the pine, my limbs droop,
as I watch a shirtless man's
snowy torso issue back and forth.
The balcony is being broomed
in preparation for night's arrival.
Sunlight gilds a western cloud
that's sinking terrace by terrace,
summoning the trees
like mysterious men in doorways
or columns to some temple
that time has only claimed,
so far, in terms of capitals.
Before the shirtless man is consumed
by his apartment, the air explodes
with starlings like the negative
of a fireworks display—one briefly parallels
a descending jet. A few seconds later,
I spy the man at his window
with his smocked wife standing at a gas ring,
and imagine, as with an ellipsis in a verse,
what it was made the second meaning
emerge from the first.

Scenes on an Obelisk

The people across raise the flag of their laundry.
A cypress blocks St. Peter better than atheism.
Little bits of animation link up
into archipelagoes: beetles are the traffic
up and down a trunk, the trunk forking
in time to wave alike over a passing car
and a rooftop full of aerials.
All that was spirit seems naturalism
caught in the light.
A cross-dressed monk feeds the poor
cats of his block from a can.
Their satisfaction leaves them mild
for the morning, as he slips behind
a human-dwarfing door, exchanging sunlight
for a dark hallway's eroded slate,
and the darkness takes him
before the perspective does.

Such as Stone

A man on the pavement sweeps
dust down an incline, "the dust cure,"
someone calls it, as more dust behind him
rising from a construction pit
gets a ride from windshields and farings.
The silhouette of an old woman
framed more delicately than a Giotto
becomes the profile of a sink
which flares, in turn, into a sunburst.
Thus did mannerism acquire a bad name,
but not among pots and pans
nor a porch's *disjecta membra*—
urns, ladder, hoses, tables—
for which regulation is greeted
with the inert's equivalent of a shrug.
Nor among pigeons whose sameness
imposes upon nothing, taking nothing
as text. Rooting among tiles,
bobbing under cars, they almost remember
their squeaky pinions' logical finale.
But of escaping stone there is no end,
nor of finding it where air would be,
the lofty reaches, where a little dust
scouts the spaces, doing what air does
when speech and exhalations
move it off the stone.

Sun on Stucco

Clouds little and far surrender to the space
in which they made their way—innocents
sauntering down the sidewalk toward
the main drag. I come back to witness
that progress with the *amor fati* of a painter
obsessed with the meager objects of his still life.
Noon light exposes the pine's hairy particulars,
but it's from underneath the eye acquires the system:
boughs fork like learning to related branches,
then specialize as studded twigs, at the endmost
of which small bouquets of needles are launched
in the dappling by the merest touch
of wind. The sun plays painter again
on the apartment opposite, bringing
up its familiar hue that reminds one
of its debt to earth, whereas the contrary
was the rule: our glaring debt to far powers
requiring such gratitude that eventually the eyes
glazed over, or, as in a child's prayer, we
squeezed them so tight the stars came out.

Terraces

Having overcome ordinary ground,
weeds sprouted from ceiling tiles
and turned golden by the afternoon sun
rattle soundlessly over the terrace roof.
Beneath, an awning has not seen fit
to ripple according to the same breeze.
Light divides its vertical gray stripes
into two registers, beneath which,
a darkened glass door obscures
the absence of its occupant who has left,
instead, two blooming windowpots.
Iron girds the whole, which works,
with the exception of flesh,
as the only substance qualified
to address stone as an equal. Meanwhile,
with mass proportional to their care,
a husband and wife emerge and hose
each of their nine pots in turn,
the last triggering a calico's dash
to the lethal ledge that faces
the apartment just now catching the sun's
most horizontal effect, dispersing shadow
to reveal the frank face of habitation
closed. But by now, wind
and awning have reached an understanding
so that despite the filled streets,
when an ambulance's stuck-record
seems merely comic in the gridlock,
it is possible in fact to imagine
that love was the crown held out
to the anonymity of agents
in the most intractable of struggles.

The Digs

An archaeologist said the garden paintings
were preserved when the building collapsed.
We were moving into a new phase
like an industrial plant or an ordinary
moon. The queen was late twenties—
already old, already mother to a child
grown big enough to weather a dynasty.
We stood on either side of a new trench
and heard how the hanging gardens
descended all the way to the ground level
of a distant past; how she could see
the capital from her country villa.
Useful, too, when her new husband
wished to visit—but keep an eye on things.
The garden paintings that brightened her
when she walked underground were now
the glories of the state museum. In sorrow
and quick surprise, I saw the two figures
of women on either side of Pluto's garden
joined at the brink, while butterflies
of that pale field above *caput mundi*
probed oleander and fled the stone.

The Temple

Stepping out of bed I discovered
my father's foot at the end of my leg.
It did nothing to lessen the weight
or distribute the bruises, as I moved
across the room and out over the marble.
There was no wind yet and the day
was heating up: clouds looked self-effacing.
So I was drawn to the stone, the marble,
and the brick, which refused to give up
the night frozen in their veins.
But these returned me to the bruises,
the bones pulverized to chalk,
to the penitential steepness
of steps leading to the temple,
where my type stood on generic feet
as had thousands before, and the self
stood with it, like a public defender.

The Thrush

Where concrete terraces give way
to wood, a thrush lies in wait. One
inexplicable hop, and it nears the pine's
swaying crown, where sky-blue,
like the color of a rescue squad,
takes over. The bird looks up, then
regards me, tilts its head, then flies
to a fir in the next yard. Nearby,
a Roman wall's reverse groove
delineates nothing of interest
to feathers and beaks. Apartments
defend themselves with shutters
pulled to block any barbarian eyes
that would scan their loggias. The day
otherwise peels and the sun destroys.
Only green remains as monumental
as the bird asserts, as it flies from patch
to patch, and its song, likewise,
moves from description to calling.

Under Cancer

On his birthday, my father the idea
greets my mother the flesh in a dream.
My father the stone draws me up a foreign hill
where a keyhole focuses an arbor
on a basilica in which he will not be found
or remembered. My father the wind
gives my face what is denied both the foot
and the mind, sweeping its words with a hand
broom, among which will be found,
like a nugget, his caesura.
Then I pause, drawing breath,
and walk to the ledge where my father
the evening greets me in the darkening
branches of a pine.

Untitled Landscape

Hills join quickly so as to prevent a valley.
Clouds hang like bell pulls over a hill house,
its high windows dismissing the escarpment,
orchard, road, and mown wheat falling
from its field of vision. Its eyes are fixed
on air itself ending, at its farthest point,
with faintly blue, featureless horizons ready
to convert to sky. First wasps, then swallows
map circular routes drooping and soaring
through the gulf. Poppies flutter
enough to draw a butterfly in fellow-feeling
adding its sheet-white to their washed-out red.
Stacked rocks let ants scale the villa.
Moving in diagonal single-file, they cross
the north face miles before the nearest town's
nesting clutter and disappear utterly into the stone.

After Rain

A ten-mile cloud lies between valley
and mountaintop. Bars of mist, cypress-sized
float up the hill like ghostly caryatids.
Haters of atmosphere, ants pick up
along the stone, and some birds begin
their cross-valley inquiries, rain having taken
the white noise with it into the ground.
Grass starts to dry. It's only a matter
of time now. Horizon-topping clouds,
caught in a spider web, fall
after a single, vestigial sweep of light
pulls the plug on their underglow.
The contrast between green and its absence
can no longer show what the difference
stood for, that presence stepping forward,
that clarity after excuse.

A Suburb Away

Curtains fly out of doorways
like chained guard dogs. Sunlight's
impartiality soon lulls objects
into accepting plumb and flat as house rules.
Monotony extends a cement hand
as eager in its way to pin epochs
to its lapel as the sky is to shrink pedestrians
until perspective tweezers them out of existence,
a bored gorilla foraging its mate for fleas.
The afternoon hours pass in review,
the musty folds of their togas carrying
the librarian's off-color thoughts the same
as the bartender's forgivable fantasies
to be completed in the oblivion of the foot,
which is awake, and doing stone's bidding.

Bar Gianicolo

A skull with a mustache and wig
carries on a conversation with a stopped
motorist. Two coffees gesture
to each other, while the heads beside them
gibber in English. Police outside
a minor embassy soothe their toylike Uzis,
too young to remember how the *Brigate Rosse*
smashed columns as easily as legs.
No one to cap you now, just the looks
that hold you responsible
for watching a fly circle a bust
when the merriment is scheduled,
and three tenors promised for every block,
for holding private beliefs and opinions
about the naturalist's monkey,
that the camera catches leaping
from the top of its little house
to the shoulder of its master.

End of Sight

At first I thought of the leaves:
soon only backlit, except for streetlamps'
ambient blank. But then I noticed
cars moving between trees
and on the next block, porch lights
and lighted windows half given
over to blinds. Finally the last
in the harvest of lightning bugs—
just one or two, really, like tugboats
into some depth (once a regression
of poppies swallowed by the infinite)—
went out in time to draw the ear in
to the soughing of the treetops
and a private plane somewhere,
invisible, pulling its weight.
And that pulled the eyes after it, up,
beyond the darkened green to the smooth,
featureless presence of the sky,
until they were finally on their own
and useless at the same time,
as if the end of sight were
the point of sight.

Frescoes Underground

Barely painted, anonymous,
these saints merely beam
from their haloes like old egg yolks
making their peace with white.
Stone overpowers sound too.
The air, though cool, is inert. This
is what Dante meant, the winning
paralysis that sets in, especially above
ground where we trifle with brick
and play with rock, dragging a finger
erotically across a marble vein.
The saints still gesture, though
without pressure. Street level is above
eye-level now. I feel like a pimpernel
seen once from an ambulatory.
Then hairline cracks mapping their faces,
like veins in an old woman's thighs,
secure their kinship with earth.

On the Way to the Basilica

In the last terrace one can see
a maid hold a water can over
window boxes too dark to make out
clearly. Judging from apartments
farther down the perspective alley,
they're probably molded concrete
heavy with orchid and bougainvillea.
But invisibility takes care of surmises
and content joins style on the way
to the basilica, where priest
and people raise eyes to the tiny host,
before resuming their places in the realm
and administration of Lord Pluto.

from

Cloud Journal

(2008)

from *Sonnets to Hamlet*

Note:
On September 3, 1991, a fire in the Imperial Foods chicken
processing plant in Hamlet, North Carolina killed
twenty-five people, predominantly single, black females,
and injured fifty. Fire doors at the plant had been
padlocked to prevent theft. Though most were found
dead clumped around the fire door, another group
escaped to the freezer where they froze. Imperial Foods
produced nuggets for Shoney's, Wendy's and other fast
food restaurants. Hamlet, running along the pine woods
and Sandhills next to the South Carolina border, is the
birthplace of jazz saxophonist John Coltrane.

*

Dragonfly September, birdsong is boilerplate.
The stir of heat, like a clothesline's wave
keeps horizons indistinct: you suffocate.
An indigenous butterfly leaves the grave
to flit in children's connect-the-dots down
cemetery lanes to haloed fields.
Time that is everything lies in the unseen;
a flick of its toad's tongue yields
only one tiny spire-skewered prize.
Nearby the last cougar parts the weeds
leveling real estate with the same enterprise
that measures its life-dream in overloads,
where predator's eye and victim's throat
hold silence in place as you would a coat.

*

The rasps of crows spread along the sky,
each fresh surge a makeshift marker
birds make up, through which they glide
moments later like wit through a letter
when words make their nomadic way
across a page's sense-resistant desert.
Poor south, still and ever about to be
that page, opting for a markdown version
of self first and then of place, schooled
to set things apart, to cloak coercion,
to see, before they burn, factories retooled.
I remembered Southwell's babe. In that version,
Everyman and Christ merged in poetic last breath:
No upgrade for the Savior, but a plus for death.

*

A voice urges us to the back of the house
where, cool and framed, away from the street,
books that were useful sit up without use,
while books that helped no one meet
themselves in ways not of their choosing.
The sound of an unidentified bird maps
the separation of a life from its word: losing
half as it flies over marsh nettles
leading to the moment of absorption
when sky again previews the familiar deep.
The same bird, up for adoption,
finds care more than he could keep.
It is like the ceremonial passing of a cup
whose emptiness is wine, and that taken up.

*

Could I not have caught the burning oil?
The hand makes a vessel fast enough.
When the suicide hoists the silent barrel
to his soft temple, am I then too rough
a being to sense the click a continent's length
away? Away. The hand in sweeping points
to a grassy hillside where the knotted strength
of five men gone to ground with cracking joints
could not force one dirt crumb to give up
its earthly allegiance. Guilt pins its shadow-cape
to my posture made poor by pushing the cup
back across the table to my willing ape,
who can never hurt for what he doesn't feel,
tapping hard earth with his padded heel.

*

But of the face let it be said how far
that index suppresses thought on its way
to evanescence like a coded signal to a star
burning so hot it turns back any ray
presuming to disembark as an event.
Just so the dark eyes look actively out,
as Plato said, already their sacrament
with earth that bore them and now bears them out:
eye-beams not sight until, locked on,
they partake of the seen. Not stopping there
they travel on until participation
gives way to the Nirvana of pure despair,
as cinders become the last emanation of a spark.
The last thing a brown eye sees is dark.

*

Soon after the fire, long days of rain,
draperies unmoving in dark Victorian rooms
with silk tassels and clouded plaster stains.
In the distance, occasional thunder booms.
The strap-hanging, leaf-drooping water drop
replaces fire's *consummatum est*,
challenges the stone directly, rots the crop
dilutes a tincture, dissolves a nest.
The sound of continuous rain is not unlike
that of fire, but muffled, alluvial,
able to overwhelm, but unable to strike,
its method erosion, its path arterial.
Rain on a window knows the tenant's gone,
makes its way to ground and buried bone.

*

After the dead, the greater bequests of death
spread over time the way a field changes,
as light swept days alter the hare's breath
before it starts, spawning as many dangers
as it charges from. A scene from *No Exit*
in which the god of nature punishes green
for its destination as brown and stacks it
like the trash it is, to seem rather than to be
seen, a horde of rot with garter snake
for dragon. And no savior appears, except
memory, the gardener leaning on her rake
as a cloud drifts through a ruin's transept
window, hypnotic as a smoke ring,
and meaningless as suffering.

*

I lie, but without waiting. That storm
of a distant day blew down my bones,
fed my brain through the canal of the worm
piecemeal, cemented my ear to clef-tones.
Time and cloud alike sweep by above
the humidor of skull from whose space
no neuron travels a pilgrimage of love,
no eye-beam penetrates the flap of face
still demurely sheeting the stubborn bone.
The "I" tears loose, begins a drift
not unlike the spools of smoke blown
that merge with cloud cover and lift
the last prayer-wave, like a rising pitch,
to blue, while body works the ditch.

*

There is no inwardness like this:
floor after human floor collapsing,
pipes and fittings, miles of artifice
melted into the original mash of being,
selves exiled into the surrounding wood
like stuttered jokes, revenants with no more
ability to nourish than perishable goods
miles from the hungry. The locked door
stands guarantee to the role of matter.
Smoke like an idea's shadow occupying
all the room, shelves sway and shatter.
Wind going after is like the body's dying
into the body of a growing text,
each story pressing rapidly over the next.

*

One foot on fire-ant dirt, and the mound
seethes, as the tiny warriors spread
a teeming, liquid shadow over the ground,
jealous ghost, certain sponsor of the dead
were he to appear. He? It is genderless
as an avalanche, indifferent, wild to plunder.
The image of fire yanks me from my dress.
I would be, though dead, defender.
Webbed in crows, cured, my sternum-shield
earth-ripped, enemy of consummation.
Leaving the bone-case, rot-peeled,
I would move directly to my station.
Some of fire would fill me to the good
if, in my inwardness and death, l stood.

*

A Love Supreme

Five minutes and thirty seconds into it,
the reed shrieks, you can feel the swell
galvanize the body with the grain split
and two columns of air competing for the bell.
A love supreme indeed, to hear the crash
as postlude to the whole on which was made
idea and life together, there and back.
Only after such sundering did the raid
toppling the gaudy tombstones make sense.
But down they went, and it was as if music
itself reversed the oracle and poured down vents
to bring sound to Hades where only the trick
of water dripping on itself recalled
how tightly was that kingdom roofed and walled.

*

The dragonfly uproots the hummingbird;
the locust, the mower. Late summer
in the trees. The seen shares with the heard.
They must count the dead who count ships.
High shimmering leafage proposes its system.
Magnolia dainty as fleur-de-lis slips
from view: no tropism left to hold them
in sunlight's indifferent path before the blade
of shadow shutters the bright grass tight
and trees swell to hold the shade
before their double, now their freight.
High clouds move from elegy to learn
that blue again from which all epics burn.

from Cloud Journal

in memory of my mother, 1924–2004

*

All winter long a brown vine holds
like shoe leather; by April, extends
its captain's telescope, and where trunk bends
snaps a length of coil to bark while sky
reddens in the rising dust, the sogged moats,
like pointillism's noisy atmosphere
where French men and women stand and stare
from the *res extensa* of their dresses and coats.
They seem not to see but to regard
each other's presence as a sign
that mass and volume both lose cast
when people, like trees, close hard,
and the intricate scrawl of the vine
plants its fringe on the classical bust.

*

Where is the cardinal who set his flame
below the window as I sat with a book
of old poetry like a Kevlar vest or hook
badging a veteran's lapel instead of a name?
And where is the rat who votes against home,
slithering over dirt piles under the porch?
Reading from nose-script, inching with the torch
of his own pupils, pellets show the way he came.
But not why. My mentor would imagine the exact
words needed to get from beginning to end
of a line of verse. Translation was his votive
offering, an ideal world always razed by fact.

So plausible readings replaced fluency to mend
meanings, and then the deep green fuse of motive.

*

Already before death you presented a skull
inside which your willful tongue fought
as lips pulled back from dead teeth caught
in their bone cage to manage and pull
phonemes thick as peas from their hull
and make the kind of sense you thought
successful writers made—as they ought—
before success plus time left them dull.
As they did. You yourself knew that too,
who were no writer but an iron judge
of infraction and waste—now half swallowed
like some small prey unable to do
more than to be worked forward, a wedge
out of which the darkness is hollowed.

*

The sky's hairdo reminds one of those
pewter biddies sitting in the waiting room,
their powder-blue Buicks marked for doom
lined up, grill after grill, as if close
enough to rescue them from the pose
assumed, having survived the refurbished bloom
of a perm-and-set and spun from the loom
of second chances, wandering out with heightened nose.
Reduced to irrelevancy by sunlight
they unravel and take leave with a flourish
of vapors moving aside to reveal the show:
that blue, in turn, making way for night
whose Kollwitz charcoal made the colors vanish,
salmon slapping less hard each twist and blow.

*

The mountains are out today, and the air
has the faded shimmer of air through binoculars.
The weather begs report like the memoirs
of a man to whom life has seemed unfair.
And yet, the categories don't declare
how feeble the wish to argue particulars
in the drone of airplanes and whine of cars
(but how round the weather in the glare
of summer sunlight). Midsummer's approach
puts the mind in view of meridians, as if
time harrowed drama as well as trees,
leaving less and few and out-of-reach
what once was both individual and massive,
if only to cull and correct the histories.

*

The flats of houses and spires of firs—
hillsides endure their human disturbance,
hives and organisms in all-night dance,
grotesque, methodical, but no worse
than classical authors in whose verse
hard pins down soft with sword and lance,
asserts and expands its circumference
before feeding on itself, to die of a curse.
Extrapolations that kill a poem can be
nevertheless true. A Japanese willow
accuses Euclid with long, irregular finger
from which a sparrow has flown to see
how intricate the green layers in multiple row,
in long branches where the evenings linger.

*

Where the hummingbird sleeps my murder
is atoned for: invisible repose is the thing.
The lurid nightmares of Mother's last spring
lie down in a flower pot in centripetal order
like frieze-petals, while below the border,
a little rat tests the patio ring—
rank tail, whiskered snout sniffing
a hunched coke-head trolling the French Quarter.
Three sparrows and a low-slung robin
vie for fountain space—all striving and fuss,
and now space signals the all-clear.
Such dreams play escort down the dead end.
There is no calming the pronouns—*I, her, us.*
Does light rest, if beauty begins in fear?

*

I put on Scarlatti's *Stabat Mater*
this fifth day of rain, this cold July
and suddenly I was reminded how I
used to hear it as, "Stop it, Mother!"
Doubtless you would have thought it a bother
that my far-flung associations try
for larger shade. It was your turn to die,
to become, without ceremony, a chilly other.
Now it is my time to make a word
four months after our stark goodbye—
another continent, other languages contest
my shopped-over grief, momentarily absurd,
and the syllable whose origin was a cry
the very opposite of your season's rest.

*

Fighter jets scream over in duck formation.
After the Fourth: Scarlatti,
Mother waiting at the foot, and the dead free.
Years ago houseflies moved to their station
circling a chandelier in looping motion.
My grandmother spread out on the settee
mulberry-red, sweet as a manatee,
presided asleep over all our celebration.
The backstory cocks its unnoticed frame
and drops from sight as another wave
of aircraft in rapid formation flies
horizon to horizon where the same
windows wait, each deep as a forest cave
or silo, after corn, where childhood lies.

*

The house lightens as the pages fill.
For the first time, as I'm leaving it
I see the carpenter's reasoning where the split
opens a dormer window to view a hill
of tin and glass until climbing to an apex
all ends in chimneys, provisional, unfit,
but straight as steeples whose aerials audit
the everlasting that would add *est* to *nihil*.
So subtracting myself, I gain certain
acuities unasked—holy of the splitting wood,
the way natural symmetry once tied craft
to its bed and scissoring out the pattern
fading on the all made of imperfection a good,
made cracks at evening, when fled gods laughed.

from
The Dissolving Island
(2003)

The Garden of Catherine Blake

for Jill

Cloud and earth converge like banners of geese,
both undulant, assimilable
each to the other.
Though I draw the horizon line
with the eye's rule, without
question, they pass into each other.

Easter again, and this sod
with its sticks and rubbish,
its whirled grasses, as if a mower demon
had whetted his scythe to reveal our grave,
is even more of paradise than when
God rose
from the cave of the brain
and leapt to tongue like a petrel
astounding the grave academics!

I do not doubt the light behind the trees
secures a meaning and fastens it
to our despair. Or that the same slant light
skimming across the boards
where we talked the winter warm,
fanned by the wings of seraphs,
is all the unendurable fullness
of this sweet paradise.

From which, so suddenly, we rise
and join the air, exalting the matter
spread below in its circular struggle,
that was our home awhile.

The Metaphysical Painters

What if, after the tulips' slow ecstasy,
the void? I see
through Magellanic Clouds of veronica,
the amnesiac blankets of dandelions,
how the dark possibility
takes the lawn.

Only yesterday, last week—can't
put my finger on it—there was
a house, its eyes our eyes,
and we were in our houses traveling.
To shovel the past forward
gets us to snow's empery,
and the green swells, in turn,
to meet it.

Therefore, I
can't tell you of the provenance
of summer. The waves slaughter
themselves in rows, the ditch struggles.
They go down because it's nothing,
not the way I would take your shaping hand,
never to take up again
the mating of beauty to cruelty.

The Tufted Grosbeak

The indifferent mother is a tale about clouds
forming and puzzling the forms,
and you may live and die
before her heart, slated to be rent, is formed,
or the clouds settle on the way it was.

Lost in the paradigm of their kind,
the birds of our garden make deities
in the conduits of their song. The tufted grosbeak
was welcomed (or not withstood)
when he came as new, bringing the sound
of what was not into the green,

where the past crests as it weighs
against the present, or the future
intrudes, a storm with no more alibi
than a thug in a nursery.
Whichever way it comes about
the present is presence,
loss though it be.

A Dawn

As in "Nestus Gurley," the slap
of paper on wall announces
the *Globe's* wobbly spiral,
the throw's replay connecting
with the jerky, departing silhouette
of the star-child riding his bike
farther into the suburban grid.

The man turns, one foot connects
with the rug, then the torso
asserts its general perpendicular.
As out-of-it as a hungover schlub,
he stands before the mirror's
arraignment, which accepts
his image's *nolo contendere*

and offers, from behind its
neutral façade, the special razor
reserved for lifers, monitoring
the condemned' ablutions
as mournfully as a video.
Then the uniform, containing him,
as he emerges and treads

across the grass to the car.
Such drollery in the stars'
departure, such confidence
in the solar right ascension!
The drill of his mother's bones
patterns his steps into a tolerable
destiny, filling his indistinct

envelope with the little gifts
of a rote life, and his father emerges
at the end of a common day
in eternity, and sets down the brown
lunch-bag, triumphantly empty.
But first he must fold the *Globe*
under his arm—good son that he is

up to and including the retinal
surface, where the world impinges
and locks its funhouse image
in the bright reflection of his look,
then carry the frog-pond multiplicity
of worlds into his own, effortlessly,
not letting go, nor letting on.

Almost You

I look through the glass and think:
how many lives does this make?
There are the deck chairs, and, yes,
that's a palm—I knew them once—
and the pool that doubles and bathes,
bathes and doubles. Until I too
am double and more, memory
a prism lighting some square—
a small pane of light, surely, but a light.

I'm getting tough and humble.
Isn't this what years are for?
Perhaps I've got it all wrong,
but I don't think so. Uncannily,
I see you now, your shattered flesh
grown transparent, and I wonder,
why have you come when I
have only this barrier to offer,
this glass and this square?

Maybe the past will speak to us,
but we won't speak to the past
any more than a fly on a window
would be, to the window, any more
than a speck. Tough and humble
is what happens: more barriers,
more scraping away, more self-
effacing until the glass is clean.
And no one looks through.

Dream Oration

Asked to give the funeral oration for my father,
I discover I have no shirt and the ceremony
is in ten minutes. Forget the shirt. I focus
on a narrative thread that will stitch three parts
into a whole for, it seems, the benefit of my students
just now arriving from their farms, filling the athletic
arena with the wary families I observed as child,
arranged like movie tableaux on their rotting porches.
Mounting the stage, clutching to my chest the few
sheets I haven't time to write, I adjust the microphone
and peer out onto darkened rows, feeling behind me
the doctors fanning themselves in their stifling regalia.
"The crickets," I begin, "played their quartet
in better days and minds. And when death contested
their songs, they regrouped and lived the winter
basking in the glow of a furnace, anonymously tended."
I put down the white pages and leave the hall, snatching
my shirt, fleece-like, from a hook at the entrance
and departing down a towpath, trailed by horseflies,
passing the cemetery where new stones are being
mortared into place. Two workmen wave trowels.
I recognize the taller one as a schoolmate.
In fact, see that I am headed for the schoolhouse,
site of honor for my father, for whose three tenses
I set the healing metronome and learned to dress
history in figures—as dreams told us they were.
In my dream I trail as close to silence as words
allow, when they first attempt to chalk,
after its departure, the body's outline. I woke,
but no daytime could repair its monochrome.

Sunlight struck sacred and trifling plots
at the same time: my poetry books stacked
like mail trashed on the night table,
obscuring a hodgepodge of photographs.
In my eulogy's wake still roared a double a silence
for the body's two bodies: my dead father
in a dream. And my dead father.

Ex Ponto

In the distance, swallows scissor
a skein of ragged treetops. A wasp
with the wingspan of a buzzard
hangs in the air a moment, then
docks at his paper condominium.
His intractable complex seethes, as clouds
begin to outpuff each other, and a storm
breeze turns the new leaves' hands.

From the balcony I watch the way
the mountains slide into each other
like the precisely made mechanism
of an old camera shutter, until,
at the end-point of sight, the vivid blue
upholds its remote victory sign
like head of state whose motorcade
negotiates the adoring barbarian throngs.

Ovid despairs from the shores of Russia.
Shall I commiserate, his urban Muse
circumscribed by Caesar's exile?
A weaker Caesar enjoins my scattering
to the terrace honeypot of another's
paradise, where only inertia coordinates
time and place, meanwhile holding
both evasions and rebuttals in check.

May: month beginning every *annus mirabilis*
even here, where reverse baseball caps
herd Camaros into the cramped hollows,
and storms of a sheer American wildness

stain the agnostic blue a meaner purple.
Cleverly reprocessed from servitude
to storm and sun, books, too, lie in exile
from the very nature they would lament,

were it not that someone, somewhere
doubtless let a garden go to seed
because of them. Someone, not me.
The task is to disencumber the tangerine
light that the clouds shade down
into separate darknesses, sealed zones
of affect, chronic obliquity, the dead
ash, after the cigarette's demonic eye.

Or more intensely, to disburden the heavy
in the name of the light on which
it squats, waiting, a mnemonic miser
of no interest to anyone beyond
the hazy outline of his own skin,
preaching to the choir of the self,
privately mad, too arch for responsibility,
this creature slated for destruction.

Inside the mind, a better mind moves
into position; its body ripples down
like a sail, like swallows gashing bolts
of light, so easily do they work the medium.
But Ovid's two lives melt into one book.
Not returning, he finally writes of the snow's
purity and even comes to embrace his neighbor,
whose strange ways and stranger tongue make all

the sense there on that other, that foreign shore.

Fault Line

Some cows stand on the path and everywhere scrub
dives into ravines. Somewhere at the labyrinth's end
the sea begins, whose top of fog slides in
every day, then pulls back, like the lid
of a photocopier. At one ravine: the fault line,
snake of rock, a slither across the valley floor.
The path ends here too. Rather discontinues.
Ionic redwood columns, defiantly perpendicular
begin triangulating the hills' downward slopes.

The effect is of a funnel, or a wedge
of speculation, sight caught on the event horizon
and sucked down under
to the thickly dark, tellurian strain of plate-
grinding, chthonic melodramas about to open.
Above, moss and squelchy ground, streamlined
by the absence of wind, an absence like a young cat
dry-throated in an empty house, who continues
to make the plaintive O with its fur face.

Redwoods and their toughened poles
measure light in cylinders, in gone-over boxcars,
then air rises to the first bands of nothingness,
ring over ring, of thought perhaps—
its equivocal shadow—like shade.
The cows dot paths that seem
grooves down the side of a hopper,
their hooves staked to the incline
like matchsticks. Doing what cows do.

Which is to give the hikers who happen
upon the thick mailboxes of their heads,
horns extruded, and massive sideways flanks,
a start. You wonder why they lumber the paths at all,
why they return *that* glare. The fault line
hides the fault like weather stripping.
Hikers get past the cows, forget them,
if only to have carried some wholeness
of their own to the bottom, then circled

upward, by paths divided everywhere.

Grayscale

This is the afterlife, that I can say this
while ivy climbs down out of its pot,
and paperwhites, stem-tipped
with pot-scrubber-sponge blossoms
shoot out a stiff, astringent smell
as attention-getting as a hiss. No
explanation lurks behind the odor
to contain its strangeness; no expression
of mine can do more than hint of

its mystery. But how happy the cat
seems, yawning through the plants
transplanted to the apartment world.
Their gray shadows rise and move,
seem sometimes 3-D. Above them,
there's the unmoving shadow of a fence
in a painting, the fence going
to the vanishing point, an empty house,
sentimental, situated on a hill.

There's a scene at every window, too,
and you're not in them, but rather
generalized by this shadow that comes,
courtesy of traffic, and like traffic
leaves, only managing to distinguish
itself momentarily from the ceiling's
unceremonial blank: the insubstantial
anytime, becoming the air of paperwhites,
painted clouds over a painted fence.

But never superior to actual ones
before which winter trees become
skeletal, clapboard houses a few degrees
whiter than anyone had reckoned—
their windows and roofs, by contrast, life-
containing rectangles and parallelograms,
their chimneys channels of access
to an ineffable sky, where you might have
crossed momentarily, the color of smoke.

Heat

Summer. An ochre light came
from the underside of a storm. Leaves
turned up submissively and shivered.
I saw a plane take off, turn into a crack
in the clouds. Then the crack closed over.
I sat, sweating from my damp scalp,
a secret sweat like condensation on the glass
of a judge who's fallen asleep over a stack
of motions. Lightning jabbed
its emphasis in the vicinity of the water tower.
The river like an arm in a sleeve,
pursued its out-of-body opening.

I saw under the green canopy of vines
the exact sag of the comptroller's jaws
signing his memo on budget cuts, the set
of the Inquisitors when they went to meet
the Cathars at Montségur, comfortless,
without shade. The clouds saw to that:
they willed it so, leaving only the seething
of insects stapled to their rafts of tree bark,
the hot bluster of wind from the lungs
of the coming storm. Sweating like a man
about to be corrected, I considered the rust
blistering the top of the iron tubing

that once supported a clothesline,
likewise the lost clothes hanging in waves,
whose semaphores could have spelled
an unconscious but sweeping critique

of the deepening green, the vanishing blue.
And so on, to beasts of the grass, creaking
with armor, yet programmed for oblivion,
or slinking furtively in their xenophobia,
mindlessness being a plus in any jungle.
Then manic thunder, crazier than Scriabin,
then furious rain for minutes, followed by
waltzing miasmal wisps. Growing legs,

the steam firmed up into figures bound
only to decompress into infinity.
From my hothouse, I watched, as the pageant
swiveled and bobbed, tethered to nothing,
faceless, yet something like persons.
Here, memory grew as delicate and faceless
as bugs, who improved upon people
by hoisting the shields of their skeletons
against grass and stars alike. I sat still
in my flesh, and this flesh reminded me
how it would again translate itself,
faithfully, into another original.

Hosanna

When I turned the corner,
there was something in the road,
its edge flapping like a paper.
A patrol car went by, and I
looked furtively in the rearview,
thinking of the broken headlight
I'd neglected to replace.
But there was enough light.
The possum's spine was broken,
the two halves of its body
working against each other,
clambering for either curb,
getting nowhere. I could hardly
believe my eyes: the gray
pie-slice of its head poised
on the asphalt, its paws rowing
air as if to warn travelers
of an accident, some other
scene of carnage up ahead.
As drove by, I looked
into the imageless coins of its eyes,
and knew it would turn the corner,
in spite of thickening traffic,
in order to make an end of it.
On my first pass, a thump,
log-like, but went around again.
I needed to make sure, and there
it was, one paw still waving.
I couldn't get my bearings:
the car missed. And missed

on the next pass, too, as I tried
to line it up where the dead
headlight was. I sickened
at my stupidity and the traffic
suddenly clotting each intersection
as made the square back.
I knew I must aim for the head,
still facing the oncoming lane.
I switched to high beams, and
the light shot out. He was attempting
to go fetal, but the recalcitrant
spine prevented the lower half
of his body from accomplishing
this. In my vanity of wishes
spoke to him, asking his
permission just as the left tires
made a double thump, and I knew
there was no point looking back.
Only in the aftermath of failure
can I tell you with what crooked
care I would take my own frailty
into my hands and smooth it
like a snake straightened into
a cane, a staff compensating
for the grade of the mountain.
Only now can I imagine a word
like *hosanna*, when self-
consciousness escorts
my hulk like a slick,
when sleep is far and bound
for woods—the sticks criss-crossed
in smoky light—for the secret
paths through the underbrush.

In Memory of James Broughton

A drift kicks the stick loose,
sometimes turning, sometimes right—
though the way scarcely matters:
that is matter's motion seen
under the auspices of imaginations
you imagined. I don't know
which was the paradise: this
inconstant perception of grace,
this flesh as bawdy as
the sow's ear of a magnolia petal
turned to catch the western sun,
or the silence of the garden
when evening had hushed
the mating birds. But I do know
it was paradise the trees stood over
when a cardinal's luscious flame
was enveloped in the ancient green,
made or found, as if something
wonderful turned on the difference.

Kiefer, the First Day of Spring

Jill's golden hair ascends
the attic staircase to the studio.
I'm looking at Kiefer: wintry furrows
bearing writing and snow. The human
last seen rising through a stovepipe.
Wind eats the smoke. So:
words in furrows, language planted.

Today, I put my father to bed,
keeping him straight
in the traces of the walker.
Nor did I forget what day it was,
if day can have identity
other than this. My daughter
affirms it, and it is, to her

a brilliant discovery: the first
day of spring. In addition, she has
made her first written story: love
and a princess, some complications,
etc., but coming out fine
in the end, in that kingdom
of pinks and willful purples.

They are colors Kiefer would
have used to suggest disgust.
Jill meanwhile brightens
some blackness that stands
as the default background of things:
mass without definition, the ashen
expectation of board.

Death is awake in the furrows
between color and its absence,
between will and compliance,
snow and language. Without action
on our part, we are leaving the snow
to walk in the traces, to trace
a design there in the background.

A few minutes down the hall,
my father stops to pee, and I
avert my presence by the door.
We are standing in a furrow
the first day of spring. His name
and condition are brightening now,
where light lays open the divide.

Linking Light

Nine months after your suicide,
distracted, I look up from a book
to see the picture window
draw an elemental picture.
A child fills a bucket from the blue
baby's pool and empties it again
with unthinking repetition
into the same pool.
Behind him rises the dark green of woods
where sunlight draws up and stops.
I think: even the image of you is eroding
faster than I can put it away.
The child rises, and for a moment
looks in the direction of my house,
the same moment at which
the setting sun takes brief aim
and its final light strikes his head.

My Raven

They say there are always two:
the unnoticed one stands
lookout over the dark highway,
while the other tears
and works gobbets
off the bone
with the pliers of its beak.

You have to look
and look hard, before the other
comes into view, and yet there
it is: fat as a smudge pot,
fanned in and out of sight
by breezes that connect
with the careless leaves.

But the raven in my yard
has no other. Austere
as a Brancusi, it perches
day after day in the elm,
apple, oak, all the trees
that fructify the sightlines
of the yard, occasionally

cawing through, like conscience,
when I have turned from
the unused window to more
transparent things. Perhaps it
means to take care of my
vigilance for me, with its grip
and undeceiving eye.

But shadowing desire, it
will not leave the yard
until I have remade my hunger
and dropped down by the ditch,
in spite of cars and the terror of space,
emerging with enraptured eye,
like one who would eat his fill.

Only Heaven

A rabbit turns the aerial of his ears.
He? The grass lays back, plowed
with the approach of…
One doesn't know what the approach is of.
His empty wit.

It is a postmodern evening in America.
It is after a lot of things. Now,
the woman cracks the door to make sure
it's him. Only the flesh of summer leaves
blocks the mystery of starlight.

Only a bicycle goes by as he slips
into the lighted crack.
The sound of the chain is seemingly amplified
as it goes from the teeth of the flywheel
to the little teeth
and out again until the sound is lost.

Until the sound is found
again, heightened, the way lovers in an opera
pass the climactic moment to strings
and lapse replaced, knowing the meaning
will be handled properly, as the last
wisps of sound disperse
into the space they used to think

the only heaven.

Safe Box

Fresh from contemplating his own death,
now that the cancer, like rain on a carpet,
had upgraded its stain,
my father showed me the gun
my brother used to kill himself.
"Who gave him this thing?" I asked.
"I gave it to him," he said.
"Wish I hadn't done that,"
he added, as he moved to the next item
buried in the safe box.
How could it matter if, with
the defeat of language, he gave it that
smile of sweet patronage
before turning the shell of his torso,
like a drawing,
away from the succeeding view?

Sketches of Spain

Times were better once,
before I read Spinoza
and felt his logic shake
my senses. It was like
a summons to a man
on his over-stuffed couch:
"Your reading this
indicates your compliance."

I used to clamber to the top
of a hill with my notebook
and watch what the clouds
do over the Pacific coast.
Sometimes I would take
a tape, say, *Sketches of Spain*
or some string quartet
to heighten the effect.

And here would come
a breeze bearing the scent
of Italy or Jamaica—
someplace. The thought
took me away and braced
me to walk home by
snakeskins that bannered
the dry skittering grasses.

It was just escapism,
like browsing the plates
in an art book: Poussin's

"Inspiration," for example,
where "a recumbent poet
unifies everything in soft glazes."
Before the snakes summon
him to the mountain.

But why not escape?
I keep returning for fresh
infusions, remembering,
in every renewable summer
how paradise was air; surely
the music of it was air too,
blossoming from coils
of chlorophyll and brass.

But Spinoza told me
life would be like this,
the best days assembled
in the mind, intellectual
integuments gathering
nerve, for the glaze that
paints the best days black.
That won't come back.

Spaghetti

I had not remembered, but do now.
I'm near the place: the tracks remind me
and the Amtrak horn that precedes
the escaping windows filled with no silhouettes.
It was my last Carolina summer
(money would lure me north)
that I heard the story. It concerned
a mill town early in the century
where a European circus, apropos
of nothing, like all circuses, had turned up.
Imagine how it ignited the margins of town,
not to mention the jaws of the Presbyterians,
whose profiles filled the upper windows.
Farmers looked up from their traces
and saw something extraordinary—
Hannibal's army stopping in the plains.
In this circus was an Italian violinist
who doubled as a hand: two hands
and a spine to hoist the tent, where
circus animals, too ancient for desertion,
doddered to their platforms and roared gamely,
where a ballerina danced on the back
of a treadmill palomino. One night
someone, never caught, shoved a tent-stake
through the violinist's heart. Legend
says a fight over girl, but who's to know?
The circus vanished like foxfire, leaving
only droppings, the corpse, and some rope.
The coroner confirmed the murder,
and a judge scrawled out a writ.

But here the story gets really interesting.
Shipped to the mortuary, the corpse
was duly embalmed, but unclaimed.
The director, protesting that he
was not in the pro bono business,
flatly refused the burial expense.
So the corpse was suffered to wait,
in the manner of corpses, for an act
of charity he was in no position to claim,
though he could be said, posthumously,
to have desired it. Instead, he was removed
in stages to remoter rooms and finally
the attic, where, dried and tanned
as an old billfold, having lost seemingly
his dead weight, he was wired and hung
in a window. Here, he resumed performing,
but this time as a storefront crucifix, taking
upon himself the social lapses of the town.
Framed, the eye-slits and dry mouth
grimaced at the Southern depot platform.
As cracks widen inevitably to chaos, he
acquired nickname: "Spaghetti." Railway men
and townspeople lined up to have
their pictures taken in the thief positions
by the brown body whose loincloth,
flanked by overalls, only hinted at the real
crux of his death, for it bears repeating
that this was the South, where,
from the symbiotic entanglements of debt
and debtor, remembrances and
dismemberments, you must draw your own
conclusions. Everyone breathed
a complicit air but at their own expense:

the unburied taking in the laundry
of the never-known, for instance,
if not vice versa. For air,
great commodity, was all there
would ever be to a story like this.
But the airs of Verdi and Puccini: never
room for them, even after Europe had
given up the importance of self.
The cadaver hung in its window
for sixty years, like luck, maybe, or a warning
that we are what we are to others, not
ourselves, hard as the thought is to swallow.
Easier to murder and be damned.

Stefano

(dead in Rome, 2002)

Chianti and vodka. Porcini tossed
in steaming cords of pasta.
Everyone who came through the door was met
with your dash to the *cucina*,
wit countered with food,
class met by its isotope, style.
Hospitality proved everyone at length
an exile. It was your talent,
after years and worlds to equate
the walk-in with the friend,
the stranger with the family
you would not have. But houses
and habitués were your line:
to each an assignable place.
Your job and life merged more neatly
than the bratty painters and poets
gobbling the spreads at your famous parties
before swarming the corners where
some spidery countess or other still held court.
In that world of casual, contrived
rendezvous you found sweet order
a Wilde would have admired,
dancing mask-to-mask, who
were otherwise a long-ago injured child
nauseated by the turning of the knob,
parents' return, the grinding of keys.

The Dissolving Island

No signs or announcements
preceded the melting of the beaches.
        You went by way of touch. You
were given to think how gravity
        misshaped the bodies you encountered.

        Clouds skimmed the optic nerve.
The lean shadows of water-striders
        marbled the submerged, sunlit
columns whose ruin rose
        to the querying snouts of fish.

        A litter of shells. Your feet
fit perfectly among them,
        much better than any shoe,
and everywhere the bivalve suck,
        sand's volcanic bubbles.

        You were returning, or, it
seemed a return, for hardly had
        the descriptions arrived when
frogs hopped into the darkness
        croaking of the profit

        that comes of adventure.
Their choir turned gross, inarticulate.
        The wet precincts gobbled up
their expressions, as if greetings
        converged with farewells.

When the warning came
to evacuate, the thought grazed you that
        your feeling about starlight had been,
after all, fantasy, not fit to be thought
        the thing it really was, the everyday-less-

        brilliant fires, scrolling backwards,
discounting the dark, dissolving shores,
        declining to chart how it came to be
that the figure and ground changed places,
        that the island slid back to the sea.

The Exploding Man

A man explodes, showering
walls and floor with himself.
He explodes like an action-painting
in black and red. Even in
the horror of it—the slashes
and looping florets it is not
unbeautiful. He wishes to be,
in dying, a better artist than death,
to surprise the surprising moment
and twist a blessing from its claw.

Consider how it could have been
otherwise: stoic leave-takings,
moribund whispers, loved ones
metamorphosing into mourners,
the prophetic gray matter overhearing,
"It was just as if he'd left the room,"
as they refold the afghan over
the emaciated knees. Drooping
in his chaise he would have suffered
a fate worse than life.

Instead, the banshee trucks pull up,
boots stampede through the house.
A radio squawks the vitals'
slipping measurements to Central
as needles shove in, the mask
clamped over the nose: body
reduced to math—but body enough,
and soon the numbers grow.
The exploding man is regrouped:
a Medevac plucks his mass away.

For rescue waits at the window,
monitoring flashpoints from
the Ready position, Argus-eyed.
And of all the things perspective
can squeeze, there is this add:
the exploding man packed into
the squares of a poem, and the poem
folded secretly into his dream, carefully
as you may imagine, being a dream.
A merely sick man opens his eyes

later, sees the puzzling bedside faces.
Beyond, low hieroglyphic clouds
melt and redraw themselves.
Nowhere are the stricken reds
and blacks. Only avatars of green.
Now he must be penitently well,
now rejoice at the stacked, knotted bags
that contain his havoc for maggots
and flies—bags of death cinched up,
dragged off by their strangled necks.

Turner's Mists

No sound here. Crickets stand in the grass,
all-sensing, waiting

for the edges of trees to work through,
photons to assemble.

Many were notorious fakes. The Louvre
hung them anyway,

hoping for the mother lode after death—
which never came.

The sky begins, on one side, to assert itself.
Its brand of blue, which in our century

stands for the indifferent, dispenses meaning,
revealing a bay

and implicit in it, ships and commerce.
Such sky, then, looks forward;

even its mist equals only momentary chaos,
out of which land is coming to life,

even though here it edges an ochre smudge
to bridge the frame.

Nevertheless, mist
predominates.

(What would be the *point* of faking
such meticulous gradations?)

You think, "I know how this will turn out,
though without assurances,

for when did certainty ever stand or fall
on the burning off of mist,

when whole fleets bound for you
stir under the hope of earth?

Umbrian Odes

in memory of Joseph Brodsky

I.
Stacked stone holds its cutout against the blue.
Old window arches are bricked, having
been first covered with concrete
and that slagged off. Swallows loop
from cracks to air and back, and pigeons
perched like gargoyles gentle into sleepy,
perishable sentries. What is looked at persists
as the seen, in archaic recirculation.

Was this the old structure of the world—
to rise skyward on the sturdy back of matter?
Or was the ambition less, the organized
rubble only keeping pace with time?
As it happens, we are sitting by a pool
discussing cloth's impersonations of flesh.
While I like the indolence of silk, you
like the thing itself, even when it is

a shirt stuffed, a movement container.
A bald, smoking father orders
his cowed girls around the water. Enough
of the centurion survives his linteled brow
and granite nose to explain more
than towers, but he seems out of place,
subdued by his offspring's gaucherie,
as if the facial bearing were indifference's

rebuttal. A boatload of Darwins
could not console him for the arrival
of the rich couple and their aquiline,
disheveled children whose nearly
rotted innocence alerts the pornographer's
instrument. He knows they are closer
to stone than he and quick to assume
the *castelli* for their backdrop needs.

You hint that silk is a good thing because
it forces one to admit that violence
begets taste, if only that to pose words
in the manner of our sentience is to have
left capriciously on a long journey.
Like lying on our deathbeds, I add.
At which point, the pool takes, like
Narcissus, heaven's emptiness for itself.

II.
In sunlight, the landscape reverses Corot:
the front field of vision bright,
a hillside of attentive sunflowers, followed
by some darker stand of green—what life
summer puts in the way of life: ennui
of leaf-weight! An unstruggling tangle of grass
promises the skink to go with the hare.
Summer cancels and dispenses indifferently,
as the artist knew, who framed golden clearings
from the nearer embrace of indistinct

branches sedged with bitten leaves
and spotted fruit, Romantic props for a time
when selves let nature interrogate their

obscurity, wondering when the ball of gnats
would land or whether two sizes of viper
supported the theory that lower phyla
traveled *en famille*. Impossible, then, to turn
the sunflowers away from an allegory
of sunflowers, to resist thinking that
such doughty sunlight belonged to the past

and that things tightened up a bit once
the creek marked the sloping field's edge.
Perhaps old fields were always in the business
of leading the eye to the edge of the page,
after a sleep of fantastic flowers
that felt you were watching them
through the page's tiny bars, and the change
that came over your face was like
a cloud that drifted behind your blown hair
and set by the roof of the old toolshed.

III.
Plow and harvest loom over the dead
and summer sunlight falls straight.
This, and the yolk competes with the fields
of sunflowers standing precisely at salute
until their fingers curl, but not the yellow.
The hog's destiny resembles the poem's,
in its way superior to the empty churches
watched over by the local police.

Fruits swell faster than a cloud.
Better to let them spot and fall, food
for wasps and inchworms making an alphabet
through alimentary canals. Like paratroopers
peas strap-hang the whole length of July,

and when wheat exits via the dirt road
beside the beheaded grass, an owl is in
no better position than the useless twig

a canopy covered for. Gnawed by beetles,
sooted by harvest's systematic monsters,
a broadleaf sallies forth into diesel air:
everywhere the same leaf claims its solar
privilege upon mountainous racks of the dead,
so sturdily inanimate that no question
can ever break through to the obtuse skulls
of the unfallen animals. But a farmer

sits in his cab as the truck pulls round
with its gaping hopper. Trailed by swallows
and a floating wake of dust, he pauses
to wipe the rearview mirror, his hand
extending to the window of the beast,
returning to cradle his own jaw that houses
his toothache, while his colleagues look on
and finish the lunch, that turns into siesta.

IV.
Trees and hedgerows, like an ink trail,
rewrite the hills into that realistic novel,
Joseph, you thought the last century had missed.
Of the three segments of a vodka bottle, the first,
alone, seems incapable of bestowing poetry. Three
balls of gnats juggle for the favor of an apricot tree.
The local group, a few feet before my face,
give both force and nuance to the evening breeze.
Doves start up behind me, intoning
the bare syllable of their stony comfort.

A blue bus negotiates the road to town,
in which the cappuccino keeps dendrites
from drooping into winter kudzu.
Neither is the white car put off by geology.
The spiral up holds no improvement, save
the way down, etc. Consistency beats surprise
in land, as in cuisine, eliminating any shadow
that would streak the yolk. Say what you will,
the mind pulls back from the brink in time
to switch either Tyson or Titian for *Lucy*.

Every day the Duomo tower indicates nothing
but diversifying clouds pulling back to reveal
a sky depopulated of everything save more clouds
and the occasional raptor touring emptiness
like Satan savoring the chaos. The wasp felt
a reassurance, that bare thermal pillar,
though once the grub's aspirations ranged across
the sexy fuzz of a peach. Epic vacillations
require hexameters designed to scythe
any shape that comes down the pike.

As for us, our best lines lie in canceled stanzas,
no doubt, homogenized by a silence as thick
as ennui. Let the thought, like a grub, climb out
the tops of our peach fuzz, for otherwise,
how keep past vividness from sinking to a level
that lets mediocrities step forward as maestros?
Existence merely arrived, Parnassian, but not
Parnassus. Still, a few molecules peeled from
the aqueduct, and pretty soon the whole Empire
faded before the more ancient snow of a television.

V.
When I turn, you are gone,
and it doesn't matter if I specify
the number of chairs, or simply
imply a renewed brightness around
the edge of the pool. No one observes
the mirror held to heaven. The sun
is having to work today, gesso
clouds refigure portions of sky.

Soon the whole. Meanwhile, I have
identified the dry sound, something
between a chitter and a buzz, by which
grasses hold forth when light eases.
A grasshopper, a like a sprinter in his blocks,
kicks one hind leg into motion,
is answered by another enthusiast
not bound by sight, elsewhere in the yard.

In the distance, elemental thunder
expounds its critique against the eye's
regime, the regime of Piero and Cimabue,
who understood that the spectacle
of the hanged man secured meaning,
which is to say, proportion and difference,
crossing the retinal threshold to take
up residence in the soft place of matter.

Now, amphibian belchings intersect
but don't combine with birds' litanies.
My daily interventions inchworm across
the paper's flatland on their way to you:
but how oblique still, to the daisy's silent,

unmediated thrust that takes it a little bit
toward the sun, after having shouldered
its stuff above the paving stones.

Wild Strawberries

Finches in the clothesline post
fall silent as I make my way along
the ground, the coiled vines,
mulch, dead sticks strewn
among darkening ground cover.
A groundhog comes this way
after crawling slowly, unafraid,
over the yard like a mist doing
its abracadabra over a lake.
Honeysuckle, black raspberry,
and wild grape sag from the fence.
Limbs smashed from the hurricane
prop against vines, and, paying
no mind to that past, green
and tender, they reach to begin
coiling up dead bark. I rip and saw,
lift armloads of viney green
to the fence and lay it over.
I wonder how last week's doe
made the thicket melt, her white tail
a flat hand as permanently trite
as a waving beauty queen's. I decapitate
pokeweed, slash that sham bigness,
toss it on top of a wall of trash.
Here and there poison oak
shoulders through: haughty,
overripe—a road company soprano
expanding under the auspices
of pecan, cherry, and fir, whose
interposed limbs thwart its union

with sunlight. A finch
squawks from the trash pile,
making a big deal of my notice.
I work my way closer to her chicks
packed into their iron tube.
Through a daylily I can see her
wrenching in melodrama,
and know I crouch in violation
of her express rules, a Caliban
who spreads his shadow through
the state-space of another's temple.
Over my shoulder bees and bugs
dart, mercurial, through cylinders
of light. Others plunge entirely
into faces of flowers or rumble
through loam. A worm
awakened by a hoe blade
stirs like the time-lapse
of a tendril too young to name.
The possum lurks somewhere who
grimaced in the headlights.
Bats sleep in their cupboard,
undisturbed by the family
of squirrels on patrol from their drains,
tending to outrage, and trigger-happy
when the boorish bluejay swells nearby.
Consonant with every quickness,
whether it stays or goes,
they occupy a rotted corner
where, below and cool, skunks
sleep, who fear for nothing,
a queen and her sable kittens.
More limbs to come down,

more sticks and briars
to pluck and drag, strangling
weeds to find and root up
so that the wild strawberries
get a chance to offer up their
plump rubies before they perish
from contact with the earth,
like apples and peaches,
whole sides that lay there,
spoiling where you can't see,
complicit with their slow decay.
These are wasted utterly to air,
which is all fruition, blazing
where the light races, mashing
the world along its stupefying edge,
earth's edge, along which I creep.

from
A Skeptic's Notebook:
Longer Poems
(1996)

Leaving Old Durham

I.
A one-eyed wildcat prowled the sweetgum limbs,
though the neighbors who spoke of him
have moved away or died, and he is long extinct.

I saw him once at dusk: heraldic, wary, torn,
the X's of his ears at full extension, as if fixed
to scissor the future's *néant*. The leonine shag

of his mouth made a portal such a as you see
in one of the lesser Mozart operas, before which
the king, with supernatural generosity,

renounces his claim to love—in the name
of his country—and forgives his best friend
the assassination he had plotted. The head

appearing here and there among branches
was just as Roman as this sleepy pax,
and so it seemed: the last wildcat retiring

into the summer branches, leaving only a clack
of shuttered leaves, taking a souvenir glimpse
with the cold pupil of his remaining eye.

His flashlight scanning the yard from green
to black, from leaves to dark air,
my father called me in, and for the first time

I had a notion that some great shift
was under way, preceded by small, shadowy
movements too indistinct to be detected

by any but the most devoted eye, one not
left merely to time-lapse caprice, but outside,
as sternly alert as the pyramid on a dollar bill,

under which a new order raises the salute.
That night of the one and only sighting,
I lay in bed, not sleeping, my blanched face

turned to the open window. Noises were
nearly visible: animals in the daily extremity
(or do I mean extraordinary naturalness?)

of desires and deaths, nocturnal efflorescence,
nightly failure. And if not visible, no matter.
Invisibility made a dark joy all its own.

When manic junebugs slammed the screen,
it seemed night's own carapace surging,
then retreating to common hollows and fields.

Here mindless, teeming tens of thousands
regrouped for the instinctive, dreamy plunge.
One night, I heard, or thought I did,

the cat's cry deep in the woods, but saw
only the red, blinking point of a water tower,
stars setting in the forest—now houses—

II.

each a star pulled down "to curdle darkness,"
as Nerval put it. It is 1954. Durham simmers
in the steam of factories, steeps in the perfume

of tobacco—curing only itself, drying
to kid leather, its liquor recycled as humidity.
I wander through a field nearby with a child's

intermittent purpose. Sheep crop
the warehouse lawns, where, emerging from
their grimy nimbus, both slave and master,

semis plod past a checkpoint. The flock grazes,
floating, self-possessed, a weather front of
unconcern, somewhere coming in, moving on.

In this same grass, I reach to pull up a baby-fat
fist of clover; pull back instead a blazing welt
and through sheets of tears spy the bee

perpetrator disappearing into heaven.
What my mother must have seen was a look
of incredulity, not of pain, or only of pain

at the aborted gift. And felt, too, a brute
courage, like the obdurate sheep when
bull-snorting tractors menaced the gate.

My dad and his pals surge from the factory
mouth at the lunch whistle, where we wait,
I in suit and cap, my mother bracing her purse

against her patent leather belt. Like a prince,
I own the hour in my ego's nutshell.
Such post-war composure, the chary victor's

evening shadow, already fogs the decade,
in whose time's arithmetic, no subtraction
or division yet make their operators known.

We cross the hot tracks between buildings
with filmy, industrial windows, stroll out
to a hole-in-the-wall named "Amos n Andy's"

whose door-centered logo melts into
a dramatic, shadowed crescent, tapered
but unambiguous. We squeeze into school

desks posing as seats, Mother in navy, Daddy
in khaki, and ceremonially unwrap the hot-dogs.
Plant workers crowd by: a pastoral pool

table beckons through a door in back,
where I'm not allowed. Daddy jokes our dogs
haven't achieved perfection until slathered

in the cook's forearm sweat. Mother turns
at this, folds her napkin and watches passersby
who cross and recross behind the reversed,

III.

painted letters. Many are black (the passersby).
My father explains that they live in Haiti
(pronounced Hay-tie), south of the tracks, where

periodically spilled like shelled peas from
the Southern Crescent, they were too weary to push
on to D.C. The story is variously embroidered

but ultimately murky: the dissonant logic
of smoking slums, chattering in winter,
charred in summer, cowled in mystery.

Here, James Brown, the hardest-working
man in show business, would come after the show,
seignioral, priapic, elusive. Papers have

a field day with allegations. Meanwhile,
a shopping center rears from a lot.
Main Street braces for the slow inversion,

as vectors realign. But some stores
will wait out the shift, make adjustments.
Soon they will be infamous as footnotes:

Woolworth and Kress forced to trial,
for this is history; it is also a state of affairs.
The lunchroom counters become plaques,

their shame converted, become what they
are now: a sift of memory, a reverse radiance,
a shadow beckoning at the edge of the yard.

Like its namesake, sooner or later Haiti warms
to its real theme, of which it is its own symbol—
separate, fiery as a love-note. But now,

heads are left uncracked; they float by
our comedy restaurant like birthday balloons.
We unwrap the remaining dogs; the aroma

of chili escapes, followed by mustard
and an acrid burst of onion. Amos leans against
his cab, distracted. Andy fancies a new suit

and bowler in the shop window, while Sapphire
unloads on the Kingfish, unmans him over some
infraction too late to fix because it is too late.

We walk my father back to work, take the bus
to our side of town, past legions of blackberry
bushes and trees sagging with honeysuckle.

Like the poet at seven, my mind slogs
through its savannas and seven seas, finding
adventures undisturbed by issues, heroism

IV.

without overhead. In the city I have lost,
the dead luxuriate. They are the bourgeoisie
of a necropolis. They no longer turn in tender

stupefaction to see earth movers scrape up
the last bucolic pools of green. They prefer
the permanence of their present quarters.

Miss Riley is dead, whose pronged feet and cane
hobbled to church like a secretary bird, and Miss Tilley,
the Latin teacher, who boasted that, thanks to her,

thousands remembered the correct way to say *agricola*.
And my grandmother—all the top-heavy ladies
of the South in books. Mr. Hall, our pint-sized

principal, is dead, who cruised the school
with a ping-pong paddle, and the "Bullocks,"
who harrowed the last farm in the neighborhood,

And not to forget Freddy—something,
a stringy hood who lurked about the schoolyard:
shot dead. Whom the Wall remembers.

And Buck, friend of my father's youth,
whose lungs his life devoured. Did they know
their leaving was already prepared for?

Did they hear the tumblers falling into place?
Did they tussle first with free will and then
necessity in that sequence that squeezes

the brakeman's pupils to a rat's glare?
Or did the subtle slippage spare them
everything but the looming intimations,

for which ceremonies were contrived where
the anxious sense could enact its worry?
Forty years later, self-sentenced, my parents

exiled themselves, but they bore the town
on their backs, complete with its heat, contention,
its death, like history inscribed on the backs

of turtles reassured by the horizon's immobility.
It's summer solstice when I look up, and I want
to amass more images, without knowing which

or how they have been hiding all these years.
Nor to what purpose, except to witness how
these dead live to vex each other's shadows.

The ancient, deciduous trees have thinned out.
I remember how they once soared into tent poles
that we wandered among, looking for the show.

But I don't know what became of the cries that issued
from their branches, or of the brilliant, watchful eye
that was, was *said* to be, and so sank into legend.

Suite for Susan Rankaitis

Rocket Lure

1.
What beyond what

2.
is the meaning of *reach*?
What will our melody be,
but pure abstraction,
parabola in a void
to the end-user?

3.
The brain streaked with thought

4.
on a rainy day, by a window.
A child pours over books, renderings.
The rain is such, he can't get out of the house

5.
for days. In his mind, the child challenges
a sodden mockingbird

6.
sequestered in the dripping
prongs of its bush,
and sure enough, there is the cry,
almost startling in its purity, close by,
denuded,
like a nail without wood.

7.
But far from prattling on, the sound
is merely bested by raindrops.

8.

Across the color plates,
the story of nomads
marches, they who
clashed for possession of waterholes;
or the search for food,

9.
ending in torpor.

10.
But the other beyond, the even more
inhospitable, denuded
and frozen, promises

11.
a transcendence *beyond imagining,*
where imagination is lifted, not snared,
dissipated; where it twinkles away,
smaller and smaller, until the ice, too,
is just a celestial cinder.

12.
The nose-cone, like all noses,
approaches space with its vanishing point extended.
Ideally, it moves as almost nothing,
this almost-nothing dragging, as it were,
the bad news of its increasing bulk behind

13.
with four hundred thousand pounds of thrust

14.
to assert and articulate its presence among
such spaces, the very opposite of
its concentration.

15.
The mature man admires
his likeness to this device,
the impersonality of its aluminum skin
leaping through atmospheres

16.
like belief itself
secure and unawakened in its trustworthy vessel.

17.
Until, out of reach,
thrusters burnt-out, spiraling, he merges
with an older music.

18.
By what right does the dying animal in him think
this a useless parody of birth and avoid it?
What have the dying gained by this?

Luminous Phase

In Bosch, to take but one example, the so-
compromised animals, monsters of their own design

gather to a common ground
as though engaged in a mysterious sport.

With us, it's different, knowing the rules,
and who are these freaks but our doleful predecessors

who, while breaking their knees on plows,
went to the rack for urges not understood,

were gibbeted, crippled, stippled with boils, drowned
in catarrh, whose last words—the names

of their sins—were lost in the rising sump of blood?
But see, they return, they are only

signs, cones jammed into the earth they loved so,
still pursued by blades

replicas of Saturn's rings biting into the hillside,
as though the way in were also the way out

of harm's way so that tormentor and tormented,
caught by the luminous earth

depict only one continuous spectacle
of procession, or the desire to proceed

arrested at the moment of their greatest abandon,
now passionless, an image we talk about

with a certain remoteness in our voice, all contours
gone flat, the way we talk about geometry.

End-User

How the sun does set like the past sun.
But mostly what there is to see is not
the image of time, predominantly,
but space itself, an expanse
that swallows up your all-too-ready
imaginings. Is space, then,
a screen? A screen wider than vision,
but a screen, after all. *And nothing more?*

Let's suppose there is a use
to sight—not to seeing, but to the things
seen. You have to account for
the coincidence of the imagined
superimposed onto the real.
And you have to account, likewise,
for the meanings you invest in clouds,
how their golden striations concur

in that mood that was only a moment
ago buried and forgotten.
So, in a sense, landscapes fathom you,
though it's more natural to think
you're the end-user of what you see.
The sunset will always bring
its pleasant obliteration, its gold
the reminder of the value placed

on farewells, on the turning of your face
to the interim darkness.
Somewhere, the whir of crickets
merges with the turbine. You sit beneath
the light it produces, and I ask you,
which of the two will better accompany
your entry into the expansive evening,
and all the other times of day so freely offered?

Conductors and Insulators

Sunset and an airplane at the sun's level.
It's better this way, isn't it, and that's
why it shows up
in posters designed to induce you to travel.
For who wouldn't like to ride there
at the sun's level,

except that you have different destinations?
And a plane may fall through the atmosphere,
trailed by blips,
after which there's this same
calming down of the light.

The way it was in the Jurassic, no doubt,
and will be some future evening
no calendar can label.
Let's say the plane is headed out of the picture,
and that means you're headed out
of the picture, too

but not without the abstract dignity
of a heavily streaked monitor
and the back of the air-traffic controller's head
not moving, remembering
that the sun's phoenix yellows
slip down only to repeat the process
as though trying to get you to memorize the image,
which, for all the training,

the lifelong conducting of your eyes up, then down,
you repeated only by way of conceptions,
approximations,

not a real fire, nor any real phoenix.

I/O

The spiral going toward hell, is it the same one
that burrows through the day? Gravity twists
all streaks eventually into curves, like the sun

seen in a time-lapse, or a mountain in mists
that pass across with a certain self-importance,
and you feel caught in an optimist's

version of an infinite regress, like a dance
that goes on after your partner has departed,
but you continue in motion on the chance

that inertia will drop you where you started—
in, or out, whichever was the way onto
the floor. Leaving you to feel simple-hearted,

if not simple-minded. Why would you want to
have it any other way than down the drain,
o connoisseur of tunnels, when the thought you

began with is the one you can't refrain
from thinking, like a Christian apologist:
hell is repetition, the thought occurs to you again.

Centrifugal Spin

Sometimes, words are *away*.
They take leave of their old jobs,
drop their plows, so to speak, and head
for the front.

The more we want—this food, this love—
the more we hear the sirens. And what is this but a fall,
or the pattern
of a fall, from which redemption is itself
constantly a new desire?

Or to put it another way: what more *would* I have

if these words were victorious,
conquering and colonizing their horizon?

Would they ever return
the same? Or would they have become
too knowing for the simple lives they come back to,
the ordinary, for which
there are no sirens?

Versa-lite

I remember driving once over Lake Pontchartrain
on a slab of highway plunging
through the horizontal like desire
rocketing to the past in order to correct it.

They have stations every few miles
for the disoriented, spinning in mist, to stop
and collect themselves, on the theory
that these collections will resume

their former composure before another
wave of mist or darkness sucks them up.
The fact is, they are various, are they not,
shattered and reformed, glued back

as long as they think the bridge comes down
on the shore. But the mist is primordial,
the darkness diurnal, and their tail lights
merely stream over the water's smoky skin.

One night, a few years ago, a 737 approaching
the Kenner airport lost it and plunged
into the lake. Drivers on the causeway
saw the fuselage lights shoot past

and the vessel, like *a great mistake*,
descend and belly into the hidden water—
some supple, prehistoric bird. Even there,
the lake was so shallow, just a dirty scrim,

that the tailfin maintained its metallic sail
above water for weeks, appearing
and disappearing through waves of fog
as if stirring, as if about to be under way

on an odyssey so impossible it would
take a new Homer, sizzling his fireword
through the mist, to raise a meaning
from that ambiguous, fated vessel.

I remember the lake like this,
the incomprehensible shelving of its layers
and the odd sense that it became
the visual equivalent of *murmuring*,

the not-distant but not unfamiliar
apprehension of things going on,
for which you were not responsible
and yet not entirely free of, either,

and so all the more it became imperative
to plunge toward the horizon
where land was waiting, meaning everyone
had returned, who had driven or been driven.

How puzzling to think you are who
you were, looking for the rest-stop, pausing
there to reorient, then moving into the turn lane,
joining the procession of lights.

Formattage

Seconds. And if you were
a refugee walking
with all of your belongings
hoisted on your back,
in the sepia tone of an old newsreel,
part of the human snake moving but
barely so—out of the city,
would any second have stayed
the catastrophe whose columns
of smoke rise behind you?

At every moment, machines reinvent
the second, allow you to look inside,
stretch both ends of a glimpse
into a gaze, a mirror of choicest moments.

The pilot comes on the intercom—
which is such a moment, that is,
the crackling valence
before his drawl pours over it.

Imagine the bifurcation of moments
into units in which to go,
like Zeno, and in so doing
drag movement itself with you
into a state of paralysis.
The sky was loveliest as it revealed its rungs
and shutters, as though admonishing
you to climb

and thus did mind and body split in two,
the body earthward, etc.,
the mind, etc.,

formatting a frame inside which
people walked, as they do,
some from disasters, some lost in conversation,
some hand-in-hand, some
like thought, which is a kind of walking
recommended by sages long dead,
who would have put a different spin on the line,
We seem to be experiencing a little trouble.

Four Last Songs

Letum non Omnia Finit—Propertius

> After Strauss, *Vier Letzte Lieder*
> in memory of my brother (1954–1992), a suicide

1. Spring

IN HOLLOWS GOING TO DUSK/I DREAMED A LONG TIME

Once more I got up and put on the CDs;
Once more, hunched in a blanket, I remembered
        the gold-greaved crickets
had disbanded, retired to the silence.
        I wanted this music
    to iron back the hush of that,
of the possum, whose cracked smile
        and fetal comma,
sick of foraging, punctuated the hollow of a log;
of the nesting squirrel I rescued by depressing
        my foot from fatal indecision
           in the zigzag alley of the street.

        I wanted to make room
for the street lamp bestowing its refrigerated light
        over the quiet neighborhood,
    for the nacreous reading light smeared
        over the nightingale spines,
upright, but sleeping among the bookcases,
        rows and rows—impossible—
    where even the word *and* abutted
        a slope of silence.

I shivered meanwhile,
wondering how the lack of sleep would connect

with your sleep. Sitting upright, I never-
theless desired to go under and closed my eyes
to let the drift come on

Since he is silent, do not lose this chance...

I heard Schwarzkopf warble the first bars:
a long time—where the phrase ends—
is the high note, and long, a keening
that arrives so very quickly
that one is surprised
she's onto the subject already,
having dispensed with the little,
indistinct preliminaries.
Perhaps it was because
there is an upward drift—a slope—to histories,
which are thoughts redressed,
going to the meeting in the expectation
that afterwords will have scaled
and peaked, will have said *the most*
to the uncertainty of fresh air.

Jessye Norman caresses
the height, handing it over to darkness
and maternal warmth, "the sound of water
weeping in the Bernini fount,"
but unexpectedly,
since we look back at the simplicity

from isolated heights,
        whose vantage makes even the nearest days
           and plainest words ambiguous.

      It is a long way back. *It is a long way back*
          and in need of warmth.

             Parmenides held the One
              to be inviolable,
     the paradise of integers, if we but submitted
       life to reflection. But in my
reflection, I saw also your snail's slick
        now paved toward the trees,
     and I hailed you in the spirit
        of that separation
(this is the voice print of that separation),
         that going with and without,
          that speech

       now spreading into a hollow
          uniformly available to the human noise.

     There were hollows where we went,
        spring-born, spring-loaded,
    already trailed by flashlights and cries
      a long way back: *what more?*

     Another light penetrates the hollow-
ness that admits separation and moreover defines
              it.
     In spite of which we dreamed

of woods, dreaming ahead, where we were not,
                which is to say
        we came into our own, but
                            but
                    with divergence,
            fecundity, difference, sex, inspiration,
        warmth, otherness, recognition, music.

        For you, everything took place
    on the level of the body, and you therefore

                            joined, effortlessly, the dead,
                                        but speak…

                            How it felt

            was its meaning
                        Even your note
    drew the police's attention to aesthetics—
                drawing inferences from style,
            gripping the page sideways, holding it flat
                        against the light, as if
    one of the last songs wouldn't also be the cheeping
            of remembered birds,
                        (a twitter that flutes up
        at the end, where art loosens
                        and passes into nature).

        NOW YOU STAND REVEALED
    as if you had become a message swaddled in quotes,
                something *about which*—like
            a remembered spring.

        But even as remembered

you stand whole, an accomplishment
(of desire, perhaps), of which

I send forward the virtual echo
from my own escarpment.

Were the springs therefore rich and resonant? Or
do I file the official report merely stating
in plain words
that summer destroyed
with exaggerated speed and fall followed suit
(the season you prophetically liked best
because—ahead of schedule—it previewed death
wistfully, as romance)?

It was like trying to read an embryo's green lips.
I tried to remember spring. And now music's (dis-)consolation,
creating a back-wave to memory, its wind
gathering the green up
and letting it down again
(*es zittert durch all meine Glieder*, in the words
of Hesse = you, deaf, moved by the same)

and so I tried to read because to read spring
was to read the *other*,
was to address the other who stood

SHINING IN THE FLASH FLOOD OF LIGHT

that poured into the sockets, the hollows,
the cranium prepared, if necessary,
to amplify the light, to sink its own hole,
to tunnel out the other side,

if necessary,
trailed by flashlights and calls on the two-way,
the house sacked by police

where

YOU RECOGNIZE ME, CALL TO ME
AND MY BODY SHAKES

because this is not the last song,
the end, but not even

the last song; rather

in the manner of this racket to your skull
that I translate into music

but speak…

and then such sweetness suffusing the empty hall.

2. September

Like the palm at the end of Stevens' mind,
it stood,
like a rose gibbeted on the end of its stem,
like a cigarette at the end of an arm,
that last thought that one previewed,
that one was about to think
with the head
that stands on the end of the neck.

Here it is September, where weariness is previewed
in abundance, where desultory fires
flicker and subside.

Wind catches the smoke
and bears it aloft like a ball of raving gnats
    or the vapors of a prayer.

        But THE GARDEN SENSES

cool rain. Out there, I'm almost beginning to remember
                    it
        clearly, the symbol of my affection.

    Is he *signified* in a flower's exhausting push?
            He, at least, showed

        enough dissatisfaction actually
                to commit
    when flowers—proxies—were past:

he feared their correspondence past. And so was always
    away: the eye saw and passed on. How many streets
        forking and proliferating
                    lay in the way of
                                the end of his mind?

        THE RAIN IS COOLER THAN THE FLOWERS

                as when I spy a bumblebee,
        and witness his head clubbed by a water drop,
                I can feel the wings buckle ·

                                    momentarily

            before he rights himself, mid-air,
    and adopts a parting attitude of feigned coolness.

No Edwardian twilights cushion the blow

SUMMER GOES ON TO THE END OF SUMMER

and it is astonished to find it is actually feeble
        (*Item: "actually" = no interpretive force*)

                among the roses.
                        It is as if a drunk
            turned to another drunk
                                in a befuddled ecstasy
        and asserted: "That was no ordinary rose,

        it was the goddamned Mystical Rose!"

            But mostly it was falling apart,
        without significance, and I happened
        to remember the ends of summers with their
self-dismembering, mystical roses that said, insignificantly,

                See, we will make you little believers:
                        reds and melon-yellows,
                                primaries, farewell!
                We lie, burnished, expecting hell!
                I noted the crossroads already
                strewn with petals and leaves

        for you were crossed, and in your vexation
    they danced on their points and skittered about,
                                and spun on their toes

            and lay flat, petal and petal,

LEAF AFTER LEAF, representing and yet misrepresenting you, doing

everything that can be done around a body.

(Adam a had a dream, which God clubbed
from his brain

using the fist of His angel.)
Your crossed arms signify a final vexation —ironically,
in the land of the dead
the sign for peace.

SUMMER WOULD HANG FOR A LONG WHILE,

the rain would get even

cooler, the garden would close its eyes.

(As I closed my eyes, so tears emerged and fell from them.)

September. I sat staring at the dying garden,

and when I could

watch no longer, when my eyes failed me, I considered

the road crossing and recrossing in my hands.

3. Going to Sleep

DAY THAT TIRES ME—
the gleam off snow,
eraser made solely of sweeping

light. Everyone trekked across snow
            that day to work, and worked even

that day, as though in the expectation of a desire

    to be fulfilled
                in the consummation
            of a starry night.
                        You
            thought the night would receive you

MORE KINDLY, LIKE A TIRED CHILD,

(more kindly? than?); on the contrary,
        your own desire—even that day—

    MY ABSURD DESIRE!

Now only a howling, like winter wind
        around square foundations,
    around bases of strange trees, escapes
            into the woods,

where it becomes one with the nocturnal rumor,
        a wind TO RECEIVE

                        time
                    MORE KINDLY.

    Even by two, it was late in the day,
            the note scribbled in haste,
        the phone messages checked, the cockatiel
    covered, in kindly fashion, the papers checked,
            policies read in a darkening blur,

codicils, exceptions, business even now somehow
                    the business of life
                                        and then
            no longer your business to settle such accounts,
                        except as the desire to do so,
        to receive more kindly the elapsed hope extended others

        if such is hope; frost pressed to the window,
                            outside,

            the procession of cars, everything
                to do, even in the face of it,
                    climbing upstairs at last,
            everything to do, climbing the last steps
                LIKE A TIRED CHILD, four o'clock
        and night most definitely coming, THE STARRY NIGHT,
                            for us.
            I saw it too and hooded my eyes, walking
                to the car, implausibly twinned, to be
                    doing that with only the sound
                            of wind
            and cars beneath constellations
                                        brightening into place

        that have no sound. I saw them rising in the window
                behind the telephone, and I knew
        that if I stepped outside, as I was to do more than once,
                and stood among the sticks, shriveled vines
                    and bare, heatless trunks

            they would be, as the suddenly dead
        of long past, abruptly summoned, on the line,
                given pause, blinking as if in surprise
                    to find such a simple call-back

at the end of such distant footsteps.

I TOLD MY HANDS, REACHING, TO QUIT,
MY MIND TO GO BLANK,
for otherwise,

thought would rush in, dispensing
its metaphorical light, and draw me back to life
and the pulse of conversation,
the business
when

I YEARNED ONLY TO FALL

AND SLEEP

AS IF MY SOUL WOULD GO UP,
riding a bullet,

with a bullet's urgency,

but never falling back to earth
and its business

but only live where no life was

PROFOUNDLY, VARIOUSLY as the oncoming snow
mixed on the coming wind.

4. Evening Glow

Trigger. Like a poem, you do it yourself
or you don't do it. And it travels
because you do it:

it has somewhere to go and the fact that it carries

      you with it any distance is *incidental*:
so many feet per sec. *It is the matter*, to which
         the creating mind can't
      keep up, but only follow, streaming
through the keyhole only to find a wall, which,
         in any case, it wanted,

                                  needed, life

         not being walls enough.
        THROUGH SORROW AND JOY
         you raised the piece, cocked
          it,

      stars watching at the north window,
by now we as brothers were *damned*, though

    WE HAVE WALKED HAND IN HAND

not realizing the urgency now at the end,
        not with any certainty

      for the song dips and returns, suggesting
         even at the end of song we are locked
           into minute particulars
                    of your imagined longing
      and my certain regret,
    pulses inside of which, yet smaller pulses,
        but something to exert a pull back
          from the moment, as though

only violence could bring a close

by bringing utter destruction, inadmissible
annihilation, as though the meaning of the poem also
were a torch to destruction, forcing it toward an admission:

LET US REST NOW FROM WANDERING
IN THIS QUIET COUNTRY,

sung in pressured tongues of flame,
as the mind, its webs and locked rooms
spewed forth, torn by the physical harrowing.

MOUNTAINS SLOPE ALL AROUND US,
no way to avoid coming off them,
no way to avoid the gravity, the animals
huddled in the hollows as headlights seek

their own passage
in some design you can never know, nevertheless
there
in the site of terror,

while THE SKY ALREADY DARKENS
around the figures of TWO CLIMBING LARKS
DREAMING, or
seeming in their incongruity
to dream the private narrative of themselves.

LET THEM,
I say. Let us already separate from this life,
the only life, agree to separate
from these selves, the only ones,

SO EASILY LOST, SO STUPIDLY LONELY, unaware
    of TIME, insanely accelerated already,
as if howling *I am time,*

                     the Arcadian whirlwind
    spinning your wits apart, having done as
        soon as said,
    FOR IT IS ALREADY TIME TO SLEEP;

    the bullet at light-speed already asleep
  under the dead weight, two masses, the little
and the big becoming one
            so fast
    that one scarcely has time to *think*
of the escape of thinking, except merely in terms of
an honorary thought, a presentiment:

    LET US NOT LOSE OUR WAY
      IN THIS LONELINESS.

    By the time the sun
    had found its place beneath earth,
    the claret lamps of departing cars
  interspersed with swiveling, too-late alarms,
 the world of business emerging to meet the night,
the tramp and thud of that business
    that added to the glow,
                  your body
    was the invitation:

    COME NEARER, THIS IS PEACE,

this caress of the beginning of nothing
that follows after, which seems now only

momentarily interrupted by the nothing
before. Ah, it is PROFOUND, as some evenings encircle
                    us, benignly, seriously
in the glow that stands at the end of our weariness.
                        Ah!

HOW WEARY WE ARE, how drawn to the silence,
                    enticed,
        come nearer, although it is *hard*
to stop the wandering, the even-now curdling
                    narrative.
        Having dreamed a long time, it is time

                                            to wake,

                led from the present

                            to the distant, but

        let us not lose our way
        but move along the wall of silence

and cling, as he has done, to the wall of silence.

Notes

Suite for Susan Rankaitis. From the artist Susan Rankitis' *Jargomatic Series* of acrylic and mixed media paintings. The series arose from, among other things, Rankaitis' reading of French scientific texts. Images of airplanes, galaxies, books, and Roman ruins, clashing but lexically connected by computer jargon ('formattage,' "utilisateur final," "versalite") suggest the impossibility of a universal language.

Four Last Songs. Richard Strauss, *Vier Letzte Lieder* (*Four Last Songs*), based on three poems by Herman Hesse: "*Früling*"/("Spring"), "September," and "*Beim Schlafengehen*" ("Going to Sleep) and Eichendoff's "*Im Abendrot*" ("Evening Glow"). Excerpts of these poems are capitalized. "Since he is silent, do not lose this chance, but speak…" and "strange trees," *Inferno*, XIII, 80–81.
"…the goddam Mystical Rose," see H. Phelps Putnam, "Hasbrouck and the Rose."
"cling to the walls of silence," see Max Picard, *The World of Silence* ("Illness, Death and Silence").

from
Your Heart Will Fly Away
(1992)

Anymore

Something has suddenly ended.
Maybe the cat looks up coincidentally.
Maybe she stares her dream of the world
outward into the room, or maybe
I do.

But something is over and done with.
It's become fact, or maybe history.
Or it travels wobbling into oblivion
where it's whole at last.

The empty wine bottles have candles in them,
and someone's moved who once
ate a meal. The clock strikes three
as though it were only that,
without antecedents, and just as suddenly
it tells a different story.

Something has ended, and the air
keeps coming out of the fan.
The songs of the crickets: what were they
in my father's childhood?
What was the color blue
in his sky-blue eyes?

The river could just about take me
where I want to go, only
another would arrive and be greeted
by strangers, accept their compliments,
endure their nostalgia, and so forth.

One should wear snow shoes
So as not to fall through the world.
This is an after-song, the color blue,
and a cricket: for something has gone down
like a cat from the shelf.
And something has ended
and won't come back anymore.

Atomic Future

My father returns from his garden
to his chair. He is worried about me,
recalling the specter of unemployment
and the old tyranny of debt. He worries
too about his legs, bum now, the veins
long since pulled out like squash webbing.
Legs that must still propel him daily
to his dried-out bean rows and back.
To the deck, den, stairs, and thence
to bed. Like me, he has no other choice

but to make it work, whatever "it" is.
He flips open a copy of *Omni* and reads:
"Atoms will rotate around each other for
the universe's lifetime without showing wear."
Sounds that emerge this fall evening,
as if no longer toggled to bodies, spread out:
children's shouts mix with the staccato
barking of the smaller, more paranoid dogs,
which in turn connects with the bug Muzak.
Finally, like an afterthought, a jet

somewhere moles upward through clouds,
routinely transcending the sky cover.
Perhaps he should worry. After all, I'm
those same atoms reconfigured into this self,
spinning exactly to the end of my lifetime.
But first I have to figure out the cash-
flow problem and afterward superimpose
the "what-if?" scenarios of the next
few months onto my worry screen
like the transparent overlays that build

a frog in a child's encyclopedia. I think
of him taking extra jobs, when my mother
would silently place the pot roast down
on the trivet, exhorting us, with a look, to eat.
Now retired, he delves into the structure
of atoms and stages in the lives of the galaxies,
meanwhile worrying about the stages
of my checking account. He reads on:
"They will clasp each other with the exact
same degree of force forever." The beans,

stunted and desiccated by drought,
hang like an old pianist's arthritic fingers.
All summer his tiller raised nothing
so much as golden dust. Still he stands
by the dry bed of the garden, at the white
string rectangle that outlines its promise.
He is like a madcap football coach inventing
Hail Mary plays to save a victory,
though the players and fans have long
since disappeared down the maw of time.

I will have to do some fancy footwork soon.
That's clear. And I know there's some further
humiliation waiting. I can sense the
patronizing gaze bearing down like faint
starlight from the end of the Milky Way,
arriving in time to catch my father dozing
off in his chair. It will hang like vapor fuzz
on the skylight until the zodiac drags it off.
For that, I will gradually grow a carapace,
or find pity in the flesh, I don't know which.

The evening's heavy sonic wave becomes
the night surf. Somewhere upon that relay
is a voice trying to get through to explain
about the bonds holding matter together.
I'm ready to record that message and store
it in the same memory register where
my father is arriving from the night shift.
He places his black empty lunch pail
on the table. He's been loading boxes
onto trailer trucks, and his legs are stiff.

I see his fingers wrap around the door
as he looks in on us, his face obscured
by the light behind him. Because I'm broke
I don't want that memory to have to live
by itself anymore. He scrapes together some
leftovers, perhaps spaghetti, or reaches for
a pimento cheese sandwich my mother has left out.
We hear him moving about the kitchen
for hours, postponing minute by minute
the sleep that will stop his legs for a while.

Autobiography

As soon as you leave, you enter
memory, and that small emissary
of yourself immediately loses
its credentials. No longer yours,
you can't recall it, or send it
instructions on tactical lying.
You may have armed yourself with
heavy qualifiers, been Henry James,
but turn your back, it's theirs.

Thus, memory. And each fresh
installment of yourself, though
exquisite, is still lump clay.
Even the other tack, sincerity,
has zero chance because revelations
have nothing to do with memory.
Trapped, you have only the whim
they toss at you to put on.
You are a small being now, just

a fraction of the old self.
Your mother tongue begins to suffer,
like an émigré's. Plainly, you
were the aggregate of what you gave up.
Now you are suspiciously plural.
What is happening to you?
It is like glimpsing someone who
favors you in an old movie
you used to like. And yet,

the costume is absurd, not to
mention the horse. Or these
others, also with your face, jerk-
ing their spears in the air.
Spilled change, their faces turn
briefly to the you they obviously
can't see. And the barbaric
shouts they make, this cast of
thousands swarming over the dust!

Bermudas

You don't honestly think this
    a retreat. The clouds
puff into cones, but you resist
the summarizing impulse which,
    for others, reiterates
a sense of well-being. Here

you are marginal. The sun finds
    everything out, exposing the air
to every kind of division. There's Spain,
like longing, where the sun has been,
    like the end of life, sitting at the end
of waves, or the truth

that lies at the end of deception.
    The sound of a power-
saw and lumber stacking: even
in the stress of confinement
    they're finding ways to elaborate
the theme of a respite.

To you it is a ratio, what a life
    would be, reborn as geography.
Overhead, jumbo jets stuffed
with tourists flicker between clouds.
    It doesn't matter that this
indifferent competition of bodies

jades the green body of the island.
      Beyond the golf carts,
the ocean lifts its glass shoulders.
Behind, the houses
      in their white hats lie frozen
on the hillsides. If you

    had a such a house, anchored at sea,
      jutting into the massive,
mystifying figures of clouds,
would you know that you were also
      moving? That your house
belonged also to the fly-away

    clouds? True, there is little comfort,
      but what it would have meant
is not, in any case, clear. These pines
prickle at the rock's edge,
      And below, the froth slips up the sand.
You are in the middle

    of your life, and because there is
      no rest for the currents,
no end to the shores and limits,
it is not enough to be
      in the middle of things that
require a person's certifying gesture.

    A sail's isosceles white,
      with a black '35,' like the price
snipped out of a book, tips
against the horizon.
      The sailors, though busy, wave
at anybody. But you

turn, enduring the reductive
     confidence of their going,
which, with each cheerful goodbye,
throws its shadow like the net it is,
     while they shrink, yawing and listing
in their tiny boat.

Buried Head

A bumblebee strafes the aged gold mines.
In the garden, magnificent rot: tomatoes eviscerated,
hanging like bags; sunflowers that were once
bright pies on stakes, bend and crook into canes.
In the fields, stopped wheels of hay, implying journey,
clutter before the horizon, above which
battalions of clouds roll up and forward,
implying the end of happiness, if this is

what happiness has been. I drag wood
from the garden pile, careful of the snakes
who occasionally slither in. It will be
a lovely, tinderbox fire, the kind one would expect
of a phoenix. Whereas in fact, these stacked
combustibles were recently the joists and structure
of an old massive wing, until a tornado
arrived one day and quickly settled their hash.

Stick by stick, I will feed the house to itself,
as I have cannibalized myself to make
the fire brighter. Up through the chimney
and into the atmosphere from which one might
spot other lights and other fires as if
in preparation. Afternoon drags through
the yard like an old dog, beside which
cars flash down the highway into town.

Following one spring-loaded with kids, my eye
stops at the bronze head, half-buried in the grass.
Its wind-washed face tilts toward the porch

where I sit. It's surrounded by chaos, weeds,
and broken pottery that have given up any sense
of kinship with the world, whose rhythm
is above all relentless, be it broken down
by forgotten seasons or Sahara-wide minutes.

Some sparrows assemble on a wire that awaits
voice to prove geography a simple joke.
(And if geography, why not time?) One darts
away over the firehouse. Tonight's freeze
will strangle the mist of gnats that floats
at the screen and supersede all this
buzzing and yellowness. Suddenly, nothing
will seem so important as getting up half-frozen

just to see the sight of that gun-metal hair.

Collected Poems

The telltale spoors
under the jacket-flap of this
big book, this lifework,
hint more loudly of it than
the plain printer's box of
the obituary page, the names
lying down to rest at last
within their little squares.

Slowly, nature erases culture
and life streams through the window
invisibly, in spite of gravity.
So the train's solemn double horn
gives out a double meaning
as it strains down the rusty track
under the Mississippi bridge.
I can take it, or if I can't

I don't want to be the final
mention of my attempts when I am
less spine than this.
I don't want to be the first whisper,
either, of the error I will be
when I lie in memory of such
a river, replaced by spoors
drifting down from the dark waters.

Crickets

They are without memory, making
up the night's story continually,
like Scheherazade. They are the old men
who pull the wool caps down
over their brows after the fashion
of railway baggage clerks.
They limp, paying no mind
to a missing leg. They crawl
in the bottom of bait buckets
knowing there is no exit.
When the grass grows thick
as the pile of a Persian rug,
and intoxicated with rain,
bully with heat, they are there
picking their way through tropical
forests. Then when night comes
and with it desire, and with it
love, and with it love's decline,
and with it death and the second death,
they take their place in the orchestra.

God's Tumbler

What perishes will reappear

as the clouds come
gathering our shadows
and giving them back again.

From the pool I looked out
and saw the green
launched out of the earth

behind the lying bodies.
What a green it was,
and no one, I thought,

had ever seen it so.
A helicopter flew over
and then a bird whose

mysterious purpose seemed nonetheless
apt. But the foundation of this
building where my life ripened

into today
became something else
as I looked down.

Suspended, it might well
have levitated
were it not as

dependent as anyone could make it.
I wished then that
somebody had been around

to applaud and corroborate
this Wallenda-esque, high-wire
fact of gravity

that dangled the building
before me like a rippling
jest, if only because

it seemed it could have come unhooked
and fallen, against reason,
into sheer air.

The proximity of that
chaos brought you, my friend,
to mind,

and nothing moved,
as I could imagine it moving
but stayed firmly in place.

A little tumbler—
so the legend goes—
when asked to produce his offering

at the Virgin's shrine
stood directly and at length
on his head

to the amazement of
his pious colleagues who were
further astounded

by the laughing Queen
and company of Heaven
suddenly in their midst.

Even from that perspective
he must have seen both
the emptiness under his feet

and the inverted figure
of himself, which had to make do
with the merest tissue

of being when the vision
was gone.
The trembling of foundations

is any man's fear,
an undistributed middle term
that the mind seizes on

in its mania
for survival.
Meanwhile, the birds

sing out of the green,
make nests,
and do not stare at their wings.

So in the reflected world,
washed and moving
like the water itself,

I imagined you again,
who reminded me of the willing acrobat.
And you were alive for me

I whom I had thought dead.
But what perishes
reappears

according to a primordial plan
whose existence I learned of
reading a book

I had opened casually
beside the water
of a swimming pool

and was implicated
by memory and emptiness
in its simpler,

perfected longing.

La Bohème

Someone said it was like country music.
It was clear what she meant, the way it gets
hooks into you faster than you can protect yourself.
And close to life, too, as when you peel away
layers of interference: clothes thick and ill-
fitting, the zest with which the hero's roommates
approve the existential echoes of each other's banter,
while furtively observing her from the corners
of their slum. Still, it's the way it happens
there in the dark: love's expiring air, reeling
out a sumptuous music as it goes—and dawn
rising to contrast the poverty of the whole thing,
absorbing stars as the scene changes. Conveyor-
belt silhouettes glide by outside, detached
and unconcerned with the fat girl everyone's
made such a fuss about. Just like country music.
You know you should get up, make your way
past the warm knees to the lighted runway,
following whatever threads of pride you still have left.
But you stay, letting it happen, convincing yourself
of its importance, as she, leaning up from her deathbed,
cuts loose and goes straight for the last row.
And you sit back while the endless swan song drills
your sternum as if it were a rock, against every instinct
that could have meant something more dignified,
before the death and the pity started,
before it all got so terribly out of hand.

Mozart

I had a fantasy about size,
that we were all terribly small
in the field of each other's memories.
That we were scattered and subject
to the direst revisions.

Naturally I want to be whole
again, as in childhood,
and the proper size for thinking
about. But again is a fantasy too
when you think about it.
There are only loose
repetitions we say hello to
as if greeting colleagues at work.
Pretty soon the trenches get rearranged,
and then where are we?

From here the cows are brushstrokes.
They should thank the stars for filing
them under the dumb-witted.
After a while they become dots,
then just a smell as they graze
toward the farther pasture, just
something that passes through the nose
like dust through a screen.
My house is in reality a *gemütlich*
little rattrap, and this a rat's lyric,
the wind that only tractors ahead,

eliminating, by way of passing,
both music and the Muses.
I wish that it were a white mansion,
with a man walking through,
his sweet limbs swinging
as he held the heel of a violin
against his jugular. Because
of all the notes, there must be one
resolution, a signature, that can make
a wedge into the eventual silence,
like the vanishing point in a landscape,
and that one note, like the silence,
he wouldn't play.

Secondary Road

Coming home in the curdling traffic
on an errand remote from my life,
turning the radio dial aimlessly,
I came upon the *Liebestod*, of all things,
right where the freeway grades into my
secondary road. With that, the first sweet airs
of another summer rushed in,

which I'd forgotten. Or stretched beyond
memory of the swells of throes,
the inconsolable, world-excluding drama
of the self. Now, sealed in my car,
hurtling over the small hills and through linked,
endless fields of corn, I felt that shuddering
overtake me again

and for a few minutes the mystery of it
held on and threw me back: that lacerating thrill,
that death to reach a star.
But more modestly, my wonder,
as the sky darkened to evening, and I drove
through the country alone, streaked clouds above,
everywhere the thickening leaves.

Stars in Leo

Across the way, a slat-barred terrace box
juts from a glass-doored apartment
and provides the evidence of life you need:
the barbecue pit surmounting a tripod,
a canvas-sling seat, nested Parsons
tables on which no reading matter
accuses the trivia-bedeviled resident.
You're always surprised by the neighbors'
non-appearance: it forces the eye away
and up to the mountain ridge horizon
where the air takes leave of miles-
distant thickets—the flat-bottomed
brush of a vacuum cleaner attachment
turned over—and becomes sky, endless
and scrubbed-out with cirrus interruptions.

It's fall. The summer-gummed mind,
clotted with incidents of its own slowing,
slowly quickens. A long way doesn't
matter now, nor a short way add much
by way of coda. The second hand creeps
up between one glance and the next,
expeditiously, like a compass
hypnotized by Platonic Forms
of northness, certitude, salvation
in coordinates that it means
to offer up on its egg-white plate.
Meanwhile rotating, phantasmagoric,
the revisionist watch apes the zodiac,
motioning the moments through intersections,
the stoplight being dead.

Night rises from the mountains,
and the grains of stars scatter the empty
backdrop. The hours honey their
runnels like water crowding through grass.
All is in the short run lost, converted,
dumped, erased but these pinholes like those
in Easter eggs, suggesting what color,
what never-to-be-realized nature
the mind might make.
Heraldic creatures rim the mountain
with only as much light as will
confound utter darkness.
The lion sleeps in his electric mane;
the neighbor's window comes on
behind the translucent skin of a shade.

The mountain is what it came to be
so long ago that no memory of it struggles
any longer in the nets of stars, no eye
lifts from its page to look down
the imagined corridor of its past:
no sight to take you through the rock.
A towel swings from the veranda
on a wire. You can barely make it out,
but its dim rectangle promises
an immaculate white, like an empty folio page
illumined by its own immensity
of reusable beginnings; or perhaps
only by sunlight—discriminate, dramatic—
far away in a future of hours,
as morning crosses the valley.

Sunbathing

Something in each of these bodies
will never happen again.
And so they situate themselves
around the pool, as if the streams
of light insinuate
it was finally all right to be
a secret, like the torsos of cherubs
with chunks torn out of the backs.

The older lie in different way,
sometimes turning awkwardly on their sides
as the young would never do.
It is a posture for regret,
poising that way as if
the earth were closer, and they
carrying a burden more physical,
whereas they are actually

emptier. Lying around this
rectangle that precisely reflects
the undeviating blue, they
simulate sleep, if they are not
sleeping, and this is as true
as it gets in the sun,
a few hours of meanwhile,
and the night tilting up.

The Mermaid

Both freshly divorced,
my brother and I met at the shore
for the brief solace of a holiday.

His eyes still sparkled
as he reeled in a twisting, liver-colored
shark and, wedging it

underfoot, carefully removed
the thin steel hook that pierced the lip,
then kicked it back into the sea

as the pier crowd looked on.
"You can see all kinds of things
if you stay out long enough,"

he explained, "and you have
enough beer." His son romped along
the planked surface that seemed,

at night, to stretch like an aspiration
over the water, whereas we recognized
its lost finish: it was just

another failed bridge.
Watching the boy, I remembered
the times his father rode

on my shoulders up ravines, through
thickets of ragweed, timothy and cinquefoil
looking for the secret places

of our myth, where no one could find us.
We knew that these places—the hollows,
the dark stands of poplar,

the blackberry brambles—
were ours to be lost in and that
no harm could come to us

there. His son would dream
that privacy too, drifting to sleep
in his pallet above the waves.

Later, fished-out, we looked in
on the island's one immemorial hangout,
a bar called The Mermaid.

Sliding into our booth we watched
the dancers bob and drift to the beery
crooning of a cowboy band.

Bathetic and wistful, but at the same time
entranced, they enacted the forward-looking
poses of love, that old addiction,

whose conclusion, later and far
out into the night, the many nights,
had always equaled, for us, defeat.

As the couples loomed by,
arms looped like block and tackle,
I asked my brother, "Would you

do the same thing over again?
I mean knowing what you know now."
My question issued from

a fictional innocence, like those places
we'd left, yet managed to carry in
a remote store of memory

that now suddenly emerged
into focus with the nostalgic help
of alcohol and bathetic music.

He looked out onto the floor
and said nothing for a long time,
two or three songs at least,

two or three stories, any of which
would do to swell the pedal of his own.
Then swung back around

and breaking into a smile,
said, "Of course! Wouldn't you?"
With the keeper's sincerity, I said

yes, my answer carrying him
again to a place where all possibilities
contained every future at once,

where girls lured boys
into the blissful, rocking sea of their arms
and all distances vanished

in the zero of a mouth.
For without doubt this was our fraternity too,
to become entangled in the bright

dream of women, moth-drawn, shriveled
with a thousand hungers so that our defeat
became the sacred ground

of a future memory. And thoughts
of those cul-de-sacs now beyond reach
were not true memories at all

but empty scrub and bracketed
bare ground incapable of being restored.
What our parents knew

we took, remade, and so failed
them, as we failed others when, through
the intimate bridge of their looks,

we saw the pier end,
the ocean heave with fabulous fish
and we were not satisfied.

Now, we rose well before closing
and made our heavy way to the door.
We knew what was in store,

what the dry socket of the moon,
floating in its chill bed, had made fantastic
in us. But tonight we only walked

back to the sleeping child, with the sea
grinding, the frogs exultant, and paused there
in the road to give the couples

the doubtful benefit of a smile,
the lunatic couples propped by their trucks
under the sign of The Mermaid.

The Mountaintop

At the top of the mountain
I sit down by a rattlesnake skin
blowing like a windsock

on a stalk of dry grass
whose leaves
chirr in the bluster.

The whole mountaintop shimmers
and the eye moves beyond
to the hills' stabilities

and beyond that to the ocean,
where cloud bands
level in even with the shoreline.

Above it, the light, dusty blue,
darkens toward the zenith
into a seemingly more acute

complexity.
Forty now, I hear
in the dry ratchetings

faint, repeated allusions
to other stories and times
briefly touching this one.

What matter? It's the climb
I'm after to the Wordsworthian
purview and the sublimity.

The flies buzz about.
I skim them off my clothes
like some old horsetail.

Quietly, it occurs to me,
with the range of hills
undulating in stillness to the edge of sight,

how naturally
and with what vigorous ease
the flies have flown to the mountaintop.

The Trawlers at Montauk

Because happiness takes a mighty
toll, the fisherman's joy gasps
in its greasy hold, just as lovers suck
the surrounding air nearly to a vacuum.

And yet, one's life lumbers by
like a trawler, torn, top-heavy.
"Built by greed, says the ocean.
"Buoyed by hunger,' say the nets.

The boats can't stay in one place.
You look again, and they've turned
to the horizon. Soon they are
almost nothing, who killed many fish.

The sky rises alive from the ocean.
Dr. Chekhov said that men with hammers
should shadow us always, reminding us
of our unhappiness, a thought

bright with moral charm but likewise,
and finally, dark. It would require
a parallel universe, and in time they
would lay down their hammers, exhausted,

and appear, hands outstretched,
mouths open, asking the same pittance
we had always taken for granted
in the soft voice, where hunger begins.

The Word "World" in Jarrell

for Sister Bernetta Quinn

If I think about it, I get lost when I see
a new slab put into place. What was yesterday
ground is now foundation, and arriving for
their constitutionals, the mockingbirds blench.
Construction cranes transform the air
into boxes of itself. Will I alone
be the unchanged one? Who am, myself,
a long box of echoes? If I don't get
the words right, the new library
rises in spite of me. This means
more explaining on my part, like a baker
who's stopped to sneeze, and the loaves back up.
Damaged, I'll nonetheless lean
to the thing that's moving beyond me.

The long waveform of the oak branches:
I used to walk by here on my way to work,
and the stylish trilling of the birds
followed exactly the predictable bird-
language of Heraclitus. Now deflected
from this square of world, their songs
struggle against the straitjacket of their
occasions, and I'm no longer sure, among
so many unsettling givens, what the debate
is still about, or that debate at all
describes what this contention really is.
Once I stood by Jarrell's grave and smelled
the boxwoods sweetening the field, the same
shrubs that had sweetened my childhood.

And I remembered that a fragment describes
how, in Hades, souls perceive by smelling,
as the fixity of past life gets jarred loose
in spring. Structurally speaking, the slab
and a bookshelf are identical. How sad,
then, to seed books with the word
"world," as if one brought the other
into being by will or necromantic power;
or book were to life as "world" is to this
shifting habitation. Instead, the birds
are dabs of pathos, and songs lean automatically
toward their shelves. Already I have to go
a new way to work, and things, I know,
are not going to be so easy as they once were.

White

The computer screen glows
with the mild indifference
of a new spring day. It is my
substitute for the cerulean
that I bring forward into night.
It serves like a Death's Head
to an Enlightenment dandy.
It covers "what-is-the-case"
like Sherwin Williams.

Midnight. The crystalline
laughter from the apartment
above has become more
intermittent and threatens
to subside altogether, as if
it had surrendered to rain,
the tapping no one turns for,
to see, at any rate, nothing
but the courtyard birdbath.

Whose dumb angel does not
prevent me from reading:
"In the wisdom of my failure,
I will carry even the last agony
to the grid of meaning."
I mean to paste these lines
to the artificial sky, to fill
its memory screen for a time,
while I sit back, as objective,

as anonymous as snow.
No longer the nosy curator
of my own dusty museum,
I have become philosophical.
Each reduction enriches me
like a quarry into which
the weather loves to come:
the snow of tradition, the rain
of knowledge, all one there.

I hear the laughter again.
Meanwhile, the cats stretch,
yawn, and make biscuits
with their paws. I think
of how love came and ended,
two storms, and yet I retained
my pronoun like a prize-
fighter, his unwearable belt.
I drag this thought to the grid.

The screen, thanks to my human
snow, is becoming the brightest
light in the room. I will lend
myself to its blessed storm
until its growing white folds
into the general memory of
what was, that other storm
I sought shelter from, that rolls
like a wave through the world.

from
The Hopper Light
(1988)

A Hanging

(after Orwell)

The earth *is* bright. And the water
shines this way through the air.
Gulls float the troughs like sitting ducks
and the pleasure boats sleep. Do you think
you could wag your whole body

at the sight of so many human beings together?
Like a good salt citizen I shiver
at the light's breaking and turn
to my inward work: too much
forgetfulness has made a mess of things.

Do you think a heart, falling,
shows on the circuits of a face?
I mean the way the wind stops just before dawn.
If so, then write to me and say
why we are not lost forever.

I sometimes dream that my bed
is floating out to sea; storks
like caulking guns roost on the bedposts.
If I take this dream in a moral light
it makes me wake up good.

Linda writes, "E. sends her love.
Does that sound ominous?"
A short drop, and they level you.
Then the old, wise doctor and the bounding
spaniel bitch, each pulls a hanged leg

to see if we are alive
or merely dead. And if dead,
we have a hard time convincing the dog.
And if alive, we must consider
our predicament all over again.

A Respectable Man

(Tolstoy's *Notebook*)

I didn't sleep well and got up
and wrote about bravery. And so forgot
to sit and reflect on the muzhiks.
This morning I looked frequently

in the mirror (only ludicrous things
can come of this!), but I was happy
nonetheless with the deception and so
snuggled back into bed with a book.

From now on, in order to amend my affairs
I must daily inspect my stupidity
in person, so to speak; stop building castles
in the air and disdaining the forms

adopted by all other people but me.
Accordingly I made rules: constantly force
your mind to act with all its possible strength.
That is Rule 1. The second follows:

What you've decided to do, do well,
and do no matter what. And the corollaries:
Think over every order for the management
of the estate. No retreat from reality

permitted! If need be, be cold and flat,
but only after close scrutiny
and dire necessity. At parties
dance with the most important ladies.

Speak distinctly, but offer no impressions
you will have to live up to next time
in society. Choose difficult positions
and be foursquare in front of onlookers.

Try both to begin and end the conversation
always, but without habitual arguing
and constant switching from Russian to French.
Act! And carry on despite confusion.

Seek out the company of people
higher than yourself, for they harmonize
with the sphere of the possible, and theirs
is an ease that time strangely sweetens.

Thus the key will be to draw a map
in advance for a day, a month, a whole
life, and as many days as I can be true
to my resolve I will continue to set myself

in advance. I must always know
at rigid intersections of time and place
how long I will stay and with what
to concern myself. Doubtless most

of these resolutions will be altered,
but all alterations must be explained
in the notebook, whose useful goal is
that I must rise after, and be something.

As for you, I know you'll never believe
that I can change. You'll say, "So,
still at zero!" No, this time
I'll change in an entirely different way.

Before, I would mumble to myself,
"Now, let's do something," and sink.
But this time, God willing, I *will*
change, and someday be a respectable man.

Caught in Rain

The rain has the same effect
on the birds. The rain which
drenched me, the unsubtle rain.

And now I watch the world
emerge from the other world
it took cover in. But

still the thunder sounds
in the distance, breaking off flakes
of the sky like a priest

making his way along a bent line
of worshippers. *This is my body*,
he whispers to each one in turn.

Birds are flying now,
worms gushed up from their holes,
junebugs glistening on swaying stalks

of grass. (My shriveled neighbor
hurries off in her Bug
for the weekly bedside visit

at the home of her terminal
friend somewhere.) It will be
like falling in love again

to feel the sky-chilled rain
wanting to press my shirt
into the likeness of my body

until I am the submissive one,
part bird, part worm, part of
what is without reason.

It will be like being
a cumbersome thing on the swinging
bridge of a leaf, naked

before the hurtling sky
knowing only the present tense,
if I should go out again.

Cleaning Vegetables

Sometimes the beet cries clearly
between the point of the knife
sunk in and the cool matter
of heart coaxed out.
Old skins like leaf-fall
pile in wet twists in the sink.

Maybe in sleep one hand washes the other;
otherwise too much imagining
would hold us off absurdly. For today,
cleaning the vegetables, I saw that
the small work grew large, brought
from random to a parable of waking.

And then another thing occurred to me
as I cut: the water took with it
the memories of other lives, the beards
of radishes and the black turnip
soils to a corner in the dark
where they couldn't get back.

Though it was possible to guess
the outcome of the disheveled mess
of bruised and roughened vegetable skins,
yet now the water meant clarity more
strongly than I'd imagined and made off
with those gathering flecks.

The feelings of misgiving flowed away
at once as the water and knife
made things especially clean. The potato
left its mealy skin, the lettuce became white,
the carrot gave up its fingerprint,
the avocado, its wooden heart.

Equinox

for Tess Gallagher

A slow burn. And then, even cells
whisper goodbye in a slow, vegetal loneliness.
Today the stem goes to a stump, a seam
along which the leaf is cloven and rains
down in this rain. If the separation
defines the kiss, I have seen so many
falling out of love today

that little remains except imagining the stretch
between the ground and crooked corn,
a simple magic. For miles
the orchards shrink to gristle and joint
and propose to carry the white load of sleep
like watchmen in the knife factory.

It is the equinox, and today I feel
the thrall that reconciles the animal
and the hole, cloud and lake, the sexes.
The ticking at the window grows: odorless rain,
but in the kitchen the summer flies still swirl.
I hunt them all, as if nothing
should learn to expect the impossible.

Negative eloquence, it has all returned,
if deep withdrawal is the return to self,
is why the fire saves nothing, discards nothing
and old blood shifts from red to black,
why maple ignites like jelly in the frost,
root, trunk, branch, and here, your leaf.

Giacometti's Dream

As if in a trance he says, "Tomorrow it will
go better." This is your brother speaking
behind the fence of his newspaper and the haze
of his constant cigarette. From the ruins
of tall men in a world of flat apples
you can barely hear him now, as he barely speaks
and the years have left his rhetoric frayed.

Every day a guy sits transfixed and draining,
his face mashed to ribbons on canvas.
Yet even leaving the colors mostly out
(colors which would be impossible anyhow)
the nose remains ambiguous. No urgency can
make it shape up. It is an inartistic geometry
steeped in the commonplaces of three dimensions.

Wipe out and start over: it's always
the same, with sameness the only guarantee.
That's the part that gets you, though
something in you understands it perfectly.
For between the exact reproduction
of this nose and the countless rehearsals
which would you not have chosen?

But defeat is a hole for the coming days,
to string them into sense, little windows
the human face might find itself in terms of.
At night read feverishly into sleep.
Kafka's country doctor: one more stark
self-portrait in which the blizzard says
your patient will give birth without you.

Then dreams unknot the old obsession
like rusty lettuce letting down its hair
in a refrigerator. On the nightmare's screen
everything works, of course. The nose
juts from each canvas in Technicolor.
A fine torture, when every dreamer
must endure his dream exact.

When you wake, over the curve of your
getting up, there are moments when your
brother's words bear down on you. So much
he didn't say! So that the paper and the smoke were
the only slice of life between you. But there is
nothing to prove he will not be right after all,
alien as he is to the thought of imperfection.

Outside, a night snow dusts the alley.
There are tracks: the self-perpetuating
story a whole ward makes up as it goes.
Only the immaculate snow could have pleased you.
But snow is contrary; it adapts until
it too is the evidence of work that rings
our heels clumping over a great square.

You return to the shocked company of faces,
each with its little provisional nose
where perfection hovered, then veered away.
Bird-like, as these birds in the skylights
glance in, then turn away to their cares,
their beaks scavenging the meager drifts
as the day widens into sense.

The Hopper Light

We are left out of every future except one.
This is a weakness that grows more obvious
as I turn the pages of the catalogue. How
when light squares off, for instance,
people will already have scattered
like bright boats into the future perfect.
Or gotten boxed into rooms where sun hounds
their solitude and ferrets out its yellow edge.
There light discloses the pathways and divides

where the flesh breaks down, and fragility,
compromised like winter trees, moves in.
For light here's the medium in which we are
the old, frank questions. And that's why
only such as saltboxes stick to their alibis,
only peeling barns, our shelters and shells
weathered like spry old drunks huddled before
a judge and totally indifferent to his glaring
censorious face. Funny, the church

with its compass needle jammed against the sky
is now a museum, the god having flown.
But light keeps up pressure on the Rooms-
for-Rent at the lower frame and on fishermen
just out of sight whose old wrecks
and figureheads (worthless as hood ornaments,
yet drifting, Muse-like) junk up the parallels
where there must have been pews. The title
says simply, "Methodist Church, Provincetown."

From there was a future into which even Hopper
was denied, glimpsing as he worked, his own
de-creation. From the top you might look out
and see for miles to boats and plunging dolphins.
You might see how its white upward spire invents
the morning air. For which the sun, all night
shadowed, swings free of that tyranny
and shines back with a vengeance. Then blue sky.
And space to paint flesh back into its corner.

The Peacocks at Winter Park

Around the curve the sculpted palms begin
and an ancient hotel, seemingly hewn
from pure rock, opposes the lake,
its regiment of sun-blanked windows
glaring down at earth's muddy eye.
Here widows, anachronistic and jeweled,
calcify in pairs on stone benches.
Only today, weather falling from the north
has left the lawns bare. Grand clouds
drift over, apportioning the sky into spars
of light, as if the season were under sail.

Occasionally, floating ducks leave each
other's company to tunnel among fish.
Their ducklings, conspicuous and short
on patience, mean that the fish do not pause,
nor the remaining mothers who turn shills
at the sight of a man and coast sideways,
in campy honking and the broken-wing trick.
They forget that the catch dwindles, being
unrefreshed, only that there is less time
for waterproofing and display, more eating
on the run, like the sporty set.

Soon we enter a canopy of trees.
There are no properties, just a paved road
giving way and tapering to a path.
Here the society worked in tiers, layering
the savannah like a ziggurat. The old order,
distant and arboreal, hangs on and blinks

as the Duster lumbers past, mud-skirted,
trudging its way like an omnivore at risk.
With the windows rolled down we watch
for outsized, tropical splashes of life
concealed in the shapes of the overhang.

Abruptly, the car stops. Peacocks
like roadblocks divide the road, seven of them
dragging their hind-feathers like planks.
We lean out, cocked and camera-ready.
In the middle distance too dark plumes
of three hens hang from the branches.
But turbidly deliberate, instinctually
without trust, one calls, "Knell! Knell!"
in a strident voice, and the others join,
dirge-like, accusatory, knelling our passage
as they waddle to the side of the road.

The Stone House

i.m. Edmund Wilson

Many times I watched from that window
over a jimmied desk and saw how,
undiminished by the season, starlings
dived from invisibility to a crevice in the wall.
The lesson was, ferocity in smallness.
This I take from your text,
none of mine. Sometimes even the Muses
stack in the tall sky like jets.

As in Joseph Cornell, every window
boxed a moment, and time stared in
from drumlin and elm, as you stared out.
But from upstairs, it was mostly azure,
out there, darting birds and clouds,
a perspective dear to iconoclasts, sometimes
including the swish of rain. Is this what
you saw, who came down, and died?

Wanted: a sky-blue life,
wild valleys brought to heel
by threshers and the queer tame men
walking the swath of a glacier.
Wanted too, a meaning for these footsteps,
these crawfish on a stone ledge, crawling
back to the river, and tiny water-shrew
there, particular and bashful.

Once a cat on tiptoe crossed
the windowsill at midnight
crying as though in possession
of a human word it wanted
desperately to express. Stepping
outside, I found gray quills
like frozen breath lying on the lawn.
You were two years in the earth.

That night in a dream I heard
slipper-steps by the door.
I rose and floated down the stairs
to a great ball and danced to sleep again,
later waking at the bird hour,
the calls flying heavily over the fields.
Is this what you saw: this blue morning
at the end of night, the end?

I too wanted, but that's nothing
to a ghost. One evening
I dragged a fireplace log in;
from the bark a tiny bat came loose,
dropped dazed into a pallet of soot
and with his mousy spine pressed
to the stone hearth, he laid out
his wings, made ready.

Acknowledgments

The Adirondack Review, AGNI, The American Poetry Review, Artful Dodge, Asheville Poetry Review, AsKew Poetry Journal, Aspen Leaves, Birdsuit (UK), *The Birmingham Poetry Review, The Black Warrior Review, The Brooklyn Rail, Café Solo, Cairn, The Carolina Quarterly, Ce Low Press, The Cimarron Review, Connotations Press: An Online Artifact, Coraddi, The Cortland Review, Crazyhorse, CROSSING THE RIFT: North Carolina Poets on 9/11 and Its Aftermath, The Denver Quarterly, Empty House: Poets and Poems on the Climate Crisis, Exquisite Corpse, The Fiddlehead* (Canada), *The Florida Review, The Galway Review, The Georgia Review, The Gladstone Readings Anthology, Great River Review, The Greensboro Review, Gulfstream, Hayden>s Ferry Review, Hubbub, Inertia Magazine, The Iowa Review, Ironwood, The Journal, Kainana, Keener Sounds: Selected Poetry from the Georgia Review, The Kentucky Poetry Review, The Literary Review, Literary Trails of North Carolina, Live Encounters, Main Street Rag, The Manhattan Poetry Review, The Marlboro Review, New Literary History, The New Orleans Review, A New Ulster, New South Writing, The New York Arts Journal, The New Yorker, Nine Mile, Nobodaddy Press, Nomad, North Atlantic Review, One* (Jacar Press), *The Ohio Review, Pembroke Magazine, Poetry, Poetry Daily, Poetry Hickory, Poetry-in-Motion, Poetry Northwest, Prairie Schooner, Public Fantasies, Pudding Magazine, Pushcart Prize Anthology XXXVI, Quarterly West, The Raleigh Review, Reel Verse: Poems About the Movies* (Everyman>s Library Pocket Poets Series), *The St. Andrews Review, Seattle Review, The Seneca Review, The Sewanee Review, Shankpainter, Simple Vows, The South Carolina Review, The Southern Humanities Review, The Southern Poetry Review, The Southern Review, The Sulphur River Review, The Tampa Review, Tar River Poetry, The Texas Review, Three Rivers Poetry Journal, Verse Daily, Western Humanities Review, Wild Goose Poetry Review, William and Mary Review, Willow Springs, Zone #3, Writer's Choice*

Photo: Liz Gold

David Rigsbee is the author of 23 books and chapbooks, including twelve previous full-length collections of poems. In addition, he has also published critical works on Carolyn Kizer and Joseph Brodsky, whom he also translated. He has co-edited two anthologies, including Invited *Guest: An Anthology of Twentieth Century Southern Poetry*, a "notable book" selection of the American Library Association and the American Association of University Professors. His work has appeared in *AGNI, The American Poetry Review, The Georgia Review, The Iowa Review, The New Yorker, The Ohio Review, Poetry, Prairie Schooner, The Sewanee Review, The Southern Review,* and many others. He has been recipient of two creative writing fellowships from the National Endowment for the Arts, as well as a NEH summer fellowship to the American Academy in Rome. His other awards include The Fine Arts Work Center in Provincetown fellowship, The Virginia Commission on the Arts literary fellowship, The Djerassi Foundation and Jentel Foundation residencies, and an Award from the Academy of American Poets. Winner of a Pushcart Prize, the Vachel Lindsay Poetry Award and the Pound Prize, he was also 2010 winner of the Sam Ragan Award for contribution to the arts in North Carolina. His most recent books are *MAGA Sonnets of Donald Trump* (2021) and a translation of Dante's *Paradiso* (2023).